Dear Professor
Carl Olson:
Thank you so much for putting
your heart into the preface. Your passion
is inspiring me. Please accept my
small present and this book.
Aug. 9, 2021
Jae Seong Lee

Jaeseong Lee
520 Mill Street Right
Williamsville, NY 14221

Awakening through Literature and Film

Awakening through Literature and Film:

Into the Dancing Light

By

Jae-seong Lee

**Cambridge
Scholars**
Publishing

Awakening through Literature and Film: Into the Dancing Light

By Jae-seong Lee

This book first published 2021

Cambridge Scholars Publishing

Lady Stephenson Library, Newcastle upon Tyne, NE6 2PA, UK

British Library Cataloguing in Publication Data
A catalogue record for this book is available from the British Library

ISBN (10): 1-5275-6773-7
ISBN (13): 978-1-5275-6773-3

TABLE OF CONTENTS

ACKNOWLEDGMENTS

It is my honor to express my deepest sense of thanks and gratitude to Dr. Carl Olson, Emeritus Professor of Philosophy and Religious Studies at Allegheny College, who has written the wonderful foreword to this book. Dr. Olson is a renowned scholar in the fields of Eastern and Western philosophy and spirituality.

I would like to express my appreciation to Mr. Adam Rummens and Cambridge Scholars Publishing who have published this book.

I am particularly indebted to my beloved wife and family. My wife, Eunsook Lee, my daughter, Jin Young Lee, and my son, Jooyoung James Lee, have been, and will always be, the source of my strength and inspiration.

I sincerely hope that this interdisciplinary quest for the ultimate reality that brings together the studies of literature and film and the field of spirituality will help all who come to read this book.

Jae-seong Lee

FOREWORD

EMERITUS PROFESSOR CARL OLSON
ALLEGHENY COLLEGE, USA

This book is an invitation for the reader to take a magic carpet ride on a transcendent journey. The carpet is constructed by the individual employing meditation, and it invites the reader to join in the meditation. Its magical aspect is an experience of non-dual unity, a unique experience devoid of the ordinary ego. On the journey, the reader encounters philosophy from the East and West, religious ideas from Buddhism, Daoism, Zen, and Christianity, and critical theory associated with postmodern/poststructural thought. The lessons of the journey are also illustrated with examples from the arts like film and literature. This journey is a quest for the truth and occurs within the realm of emptiness, the non-dual unity of everything.

In chapters 2-4, the reader is instructed to meditate on the points raised in each chapter. Thus, this call to meditate forms the book's methodological foundation that is intended not merely to inform the reader but also to transform the reader into an awakened state. In addition to its meditational foundation, this book exposes itself as an interdisciplinary quest by using literature (novels, plays, and poems), spirituality, films, philosophy, and religion. This type of approach's overall intention is to lead the reader to an aesthetic sensibility that destroys the duality of the deluded ego. The book aims to enable the reader to experience ultimate reality or, metaphorically, the non-dual dancing light world.

In the initial chapter, the author attempts to create a dialogue between himself and his reader; he does so by raising questions about various disciplines leading to ultimate reality. After confessing his desire to reach a wider audience, the author links Buddhist meditation with literature and film. He implies that these forms of culture can lead a person to an awakening by creating an aesthetic sensibility and giving one a glimpse of ultimate reality. The author also makes a case in this first chapter for the usefulness and benefits of meditation within the world, an exercise that assaults the ego or false self. Moreover, he combines postmodern ethics with Mahayana Buddhism to demonstrate the true nature of the self and empirical ego. It is also possible to encounter the real self by reading literature or watching a film, suggesting that the arts can lead one to awaken. The author illustrates his theory about the true nature of the self by using the Oscar-winning movies *Parasite* and *Joker*.

Chapter two raises problematic philosophical issues of thinking and reasoning within the context of western metaphysics. The reader learns that a person can stay in a meditative state while reading literature or watching a film. The reader should be prepared to comprehend that one is reading an interpretation of western material from the author's eastern perspective, a native of South Korea where he teaches, and Buddhism and Daoism shape that. After discussing reason and infinity, the author tells his reader that he wants to link intellectuality and spirituality before mentioning genuine happiness that he interprets as pure awareness, unlike the dualism of the self to be discovered in the Book of Genesis.

Chapter three marks a creative and provocative turn in the book because it considers selected examples of art to interpret them as *kongans* (*koans* in the Japanese language), which have their origin in the Zen (Seon in the Korean language) Buddhist tradition. *Kongans* represent enigmatic dialogues between a master and a disciple used in monastic settings as objects of meditation to concentrate the mind on a single thing and block out extraneous distractions. These *kongans* are designated as language meditation. Within each dialogue or saying, there is a keyword (*hwadus*). This meditation method is traced back to the historical Buddha, who held up a flower and remained silent as he sat before a confused and hushed assembly of people waiting to hear his teaching. However, one monk named Mahakasyapa smiled at the Buddha's gesture and wordless response. When the Buddha saw the monk's smile, he was convinced that the monk grasped the message that the truth cannot be conveyed in language. The author does not recommend this type of meditation for beginners.

A profusion of *kongans* appears in chapter four in the literary form of the following works: *Hamlet* by William Shakespeare, *Moby Dick the Whale* by Herman Melville, and *The Strange Case of Dr. Jekyll and Mr. Hyde* by Robert Louis Stevenson. This procedure represents a radical way of approaching and comprehending these works and represents an eastern interpretation of these literary works. In the postmodern spirit, it is certainly a different way to interpret these texts. Jae-seong Lee draws a parallel between reading literature and watching films, and meditation. He also calls attention to ethics issues and discusses the good and evil aspects of Melville's novel. And he adds an emphasis on becoming that is symbolized by the migration of the whale. Ethical issues are also raised by Stevenson's work about anger, pride, hatred, and their relationship to ego. When we read Hamlet as a *kongan*, its keywords are "To be or not to be?"

Lee is convinced that these art types can lead one to ultimate reality by freeing a reader from their ego intensity. He ventures into a comparison with a Christian fundamentalist approach to scripture. What is his purpose in this instance? He wants to indicate the importance of abolishing the ego by meditating on these types of art. What inspires Jae-seong Lee's study and spiritual guidebook is the instructions of the Zen figure Hakuin, a seventeenth-century Japanese master and reformer, and his teaching that a disciple should turn everything that one does into a mode of meditation.

Jae-seong Lee returns to Dr. Jekyll and Mr. Hyde's narrative and adds a motion picture film to the book written by Oscar Wilde in 1890 of *The Picture of Dorian Gray*, two examples of Gothic fiction. The author thinks that these examples of Gothic literature give rise to an aesthetic experience of the sublime. Besides, these works can be conceived as *kongans* that help a reader escape dualism. Again, the similarity between meditation and reading a literary work is evident in this chapter. Being grounded in meditation, the author indicates how to use language to go beyond language. From a different perspective, it is viewing a film to surpass its art form. In summary, the way of art can become a spiritual path to awakening to the ego's duality and the non-dual reality of emptiness. This realization is the dawn of the light.

This book represents a ride on a magical carpet intended to culminate with a personal awakening. It is thus a spiritual work that transcends ordinary interpretation, which itself is an art. It helps us to witness how the path of art is also a philosophical and religious way. Its lessons are comprehensible enough for the average reader to grasp and from which to benefit spiritually. In short, this book is the magic carpet, and you, the reader, are invited to ride within emptiness. Have fun! And enjoy the ride!

INTRODUCTION

This book will guide the audience *spiritually* to advance through everyday affairs, particularly in the reading of *literary works and watching* of *films in a more desirable way than the simple thematic approach of the conventional style.* It will lead the reader to what happens while and after experiencing the aesthetic sublime feeling. Using mainly Buddhism and Western postmodern ethics (and also some examples from the Christian Bible), this book articulates that literature and film lead the audience through the aesthetic sublime sensibility by showing that the power of the sublime deconstructs the dual structure of the thinking ego and by presents many examples. The deconstruction brought by the power of the sublime much clearer as we see the sublime or jouissance from the perspective of postmodernism (not the thought of some misunderstanding people who call themselves postmodernists and proclaim that "anything goes") than modernism. By reading this work, literary readers and film viewers will become better able to encounter the ultimate reality of their lives, or, the world of nondual dancing light.

This work will appeal primarily to *professors and graduate students* of literature, film, or Buddhism and Taoism, yet it is not limited to people with a high level of philosophical knowledge. It will also strongly engage spiritual teachers, meditation leaders, and lay practitioners. *Chapter 1* takes the form of *questions and long answers* with the purpose of attracting the spiritual people's attention. It is not only when I work as a scholar and professor but also whenever I practice Buddhist meditation, alone or on retreat with others, that I strongly feel this kind of work makes philosophical literary criticism understandable for spiritual people. This is essentially because the academic field and the area of spirituality, religious or secular, share precisely the same purpose—to guide the reader to the ultimate reality, truth, or emptiness, in Buddhist terms. Unlike my previous book published in the United States, *Postmodern Ethics, Emptiness, and Literature: Encounters between East and West* (2015),[1] this project is aimed at reaching a much wider audience. As you go on reading, you will comprehend deep

---

[1] I was fortunate enough to win the Grand Prize at the 7th Wonhyo Academic Awards in 2016, the most prestigious academic award in South Korean Buddhism, for this book.

sources of the genuine happiness that you will want to experience with ease almost every day—through the works of literature and film. You will be guided to Truth that reveals itself just by reading books or watching movies.

As mentioned, Chapter 1 takes the form of questions and long answers in order to guide general readers to spiritual depths. All five chapters have footnotes that manifest the academically valid sources of my thoughts so as to support the validity of what I tell you. The source of spiritual teachings that mainly utilize poetry go with the work of finding an appropriate theme and an underlying sense of stillness and peace. My way of linking Buddhist meditation to literature and film is quite different from those that others have previously put forward.

I am convinced that it is now time for intellectual (philosophical, critical, academic) explanations and spiritual experiences to be brought to work together in the common areas of literature and film. The main issue of this book is that we enter the dimension of pure consciousness as we read literary works or watch movies in a meditative state. The topics addressed, scope, and approach of this book involve contemporary postmodern/poststructural critical theory, literary criticism in particular, and Mahāyāna—especially *kongan* and *hwadu* Ch'an/Seon/Zen—Buddhist thought, which will be explained in detail. However, the theoretical ground is only to help the twenty-first-century audience to deeply comprehend how literature and film offer us precious opportunities to experience the sublime aesthetic sensibility through which we glimpse the ultimate reality.

It is important for literary readers to experience someone's life story by encountering *the non-duality of the ultimate reality in a way that transcends the dual nature of our five senses.* Toward the end of a given story, both concepts of good and evil are deconstructed (the dual construct is destroyed), and emptiness looms inside us. We experience the aesthetic sublime as the momentum of having a glimpse of perfect emptiness as fullness and infinity. The deconstructive and ethical reading of literature and watching of films, which is different from the commonplace thematic approach of the conventional style, will lead readers to the spiritual dimension of *non-duality* and does not require the audience to engage in a complicated thinking process. As I explain in this book, as we read the story as a vast *kongan* (an anecdote that leads Ch'an (Chinese), Seon (Korean), Zen (Japanese), and Thiền (Vietnamese) meditation practitioners beyond language and thought) in a meditative state of mind, we will go on powerfully to quest for the awakening to the ultimate reality of our life and the whole universe.

In Chapters 4 and 5 in particular, I ask readers to practice meditation after reading the literary works or watching the film adaptations that I take as examples there, although I do not set out specific rules that readers are expected to follow. As explained in the book, great movies such as *Forrest Gump, Citizen Kane* (1941), and the 2020 Oscar-winning *Joker* and *Parasite*, as well as the literary works of *Hamlet, Moby-Dick,* and *Dr. Jekyll and Mr. Hyde* that I explain in the two chapters, lead us to the true self, which is the consciousness of the whole universe, or Buddha-nature as the perfect emptiness as fullness.

There have not been books that are as interdisciplinary as this project, not only in view of crossing the specialisms of the studies of literature and film but also in its openness toward general audiences. No doubt, in the United States alone, an uncountable number of books have been published on critical theory, as well as numerous books in each field of literary criticism, criticism of the arts, Asian studies, spirituality, and meditation. There have been a relatively small number of East-West comparative studies in the area of literary criticism. Spirituality and meditation have always been important issues for the general audience who are interested in Buddhism and Hinduism, yet these have not been serious issues in the academic world of literary studies.

It is a pity that spiritual leaders' teachings are not readily accepted by those scholars whose minds are so fond of their academically thematic approach and who are simply attached to the phenomena that are built by cognitive creativity and the language of the writer. Nor do popular spiritual teachers appreciate academic thinking, which does not directly transcend the level of using the mind in a logical way. Reasoning, although it works like a map or guide book that explains how we approach the ultimate reality, is limited to the work of the ego, which prevents the mind from experiencing the power of true freedom. Nevertheless, intellectual understanding can lead the audience to better comprehend and more deeply experience the ultimate spiritual reality.

This book advances the cutting edge of the contemporary issues of the Other and infinity by taking advantage of literary criticism, film criticism, Buddhism, and Taoism for meditation. A great merit of this book is that it reaches spirituality beyond academic circles. On the basis of this discussion of East-West comparative philosophy, it also guides you to experience what cannot be logically understood or felt with your five senses—the *infinity* of the Other or truly non-dual emptiness as fullness. All these expected audiences are those who would like to reach the foundation of true wisdom, for which other names are God, Buddha-nature, Tao, all-embracing love, and the true self. The title, *Into the Dancing Light,* means that literature and film lead us into the absolute truth, the light freely engendering (as if dancing) all phenomena, so that we may truly become one with that light.

The logical discussions of literature and film that we meet in our everyday life in the light of *non-duality* would truly help large numbers of people to overcome their sufferings. The deconstructive and ethical way of reading/watching that I demonstrate in this book would not be difficult for those who accept the teachings of renowned spiritual teachers such as Eckhart Tolle, Adyashanti, and Kenneth Wilber.

Therefore, from my experiences, intellectuality and spirituality are not to be recognized as clear-cut separate fields that push against each other. They can also reach out and help each other for the sake of human understanding of the ultimate reality. They can work not only for other people in their own fields but also for the public as they ease the tension of their minds, freeing themselves from their constraints. The ultimate reality, which is the universal and infinite self, is the common goal. Despite the fact that the non-dual truth lies beyond phenomena, it also produces all phenomena whose nature is only dualistic. Intellectuality and spirituality will contribute to each other in the way I demonstrate in this book.

It is well-known that countless people throughout the whole world, including a great number of Americans (as I emphasize), practice meditation—first to reduce the stress and anxiety they experience in everyday life, and, on a more serious level, to attain spiritual enlightenment from the dreamlike quality of life as a whole. It is clear to me that literature and film, with which we are in easy contact every day, can contribute to our lives by offering us the chance of experiencing the debacle of the hero's life.

More specifically, this book shows how a story of the destruction of the form of what is called "binary opposition" (in critical theory)—good and evil, right and wrong, presence and absence—leads us beyond language to enter the spiritual dimension of the Middle Path, or Transmiddle Path (the term I have coined in order to let readers better understand the Buddhist term 'the Middle Path'). Just to mention two simple examples I take in this book, in *Hamlet,* not only does the wicked and immoral figure Claudius die, but so does Hamlet, the conscientious, reflective, and responsible hero. *Jekyll and Hyde* shows that the polar opposites are actually one. We start to experience the spiritual dimension of non-duality where the dual structure is destroyed and offered to us as the momentum of feelings of the sublime. This book explains the spiritual dimension of non-duality in great detail and beyond doubt.

Regarding spirituality, I will talk about my experiences. For years, I have been through different forms of strong and wonderful bliss, whether I was practicing meditation or not. There is no doubt I came back to pain when I was in the kinds of situation that did not please me. My ego took the form of too much pride in pleasurable situations. For some while, I was in the middle of extreme mental suffering caused by some unexpected complicated events that were directly about my birth and life. Then all of a sudden, on three occasions, I very clearly felt the immense power that separates my infinite true self and my ego. Each time I immediately felt remarkable freedom from pain, including loneness and depression. For about nine months or so, I was in excellent shape without feeling unhappiness and pain at all, yet then came back to loneness again. However, I knew I was spiritually growing throughout all these experiences.

Then I finally had a true experience without any feeling or thought. It was not an "experience" in the usual sense. I never had a contact with the world that could be called "inside" or "outside" myself. The inside and the outside were just *one*. For a whole day, until I fell asleep that night, I knew much more than clearly that all beings and things were just *one* and that there was no room for a hierarchy of values. I was just calm and knew that there was absolutely no boundary between me and the objects. Yet it was indescribable; there is no way to explain or describe how the world was so or how I knew it so vividly. I also keenly knew that there is really one true time and that it is only now, the present moment. Everything was an image that appears in the space or on the screen of the true self, and it disappears as it appears. It is rather "appearing as disappearing," as I call it in Chapter 3. Yet at the same time they were real; I was not in a vision or any fictive state of mind. Since that time of experiencing the epiphany of the ultimate reality, I have been attaining more and more wisdom to live my everyday life fully, there in the ultimate reality, as my true self. That both special and plain kind of experience came to be the firm ground of my everyday experiences. I now know that such a state (so as to transfer it into language, for it is not a "state") of mind has always been the firm ground of my life since and prior to my birth, and also the foundation of the lives of all humans and all other existences.

Nevertheless, I would not cloud the issue of this book by talking more about my own spiritual experiences or those of others. I hope that this book, which involves the reader in literary works and films, is more practical and more interesting for the sake of the audience than works on the simple topics of the life of the Buddha or the right way to meditate. I would like to talk more about spirituality in itself in my next book. Thank you very much!

Jae-seong Lee
(ethicsjl33557@gmail.com)
Department of English Language and Literature
Pusan National University, South Korea

WHY DO WE NEED THE MEDITATIVE MIND? PRESENT AGE SPIRITUALITY AND FILMS: *PARASITE*, *JOKER*, AND OTHERS

1.1. Why do we need a meditative mind?

Q: Well, the first point that comes into my mind is this. To live happily, would it not be enough to pursue happiness in the way we choose to deal with daily matters, whatever occasion arises? Why must we be enlightened?

That is a great question to begin with! Every day, we have to face what life deals us—different conditions, unexpected responses from others, whether they are large or trivial ones. It happens that your customers or clients demand you to do something bigger than what you think is right for them to ask. One or more of your colleagues gets on your nerves and bugs you by disregarding your rights. Even your family members can be people like that.

Far more than that, life's difficulties do not end on the outside. The realm of negative feelings is unimaginably broad—that is, you feel it arise inside you. A while after you feel good about your achievement, you see an unanticipated turn of events that lets you down. Facing your inability to handle important matters successfully, you feel foolish, or sometimes reach the conclusion that you are a person of highly nervous temperament. Then you go on to seek something that would please you; when you are pleased, you think you are happy. Most of us live this way, switching between elation and depression, ambition and jealousy, etc. Living this way, weeks, months, and years pass, and we grow older and older, complaining about time flying. Are we meant to live this way? Is it just OK to live by following the usual senses of happiness and shallow satisfaction? Would you not want lasting peace inside you? What if there was a way of living beyond suffering from oscillating between polar opposite emotions?

Any group with a collective egoistic desire is only hungry for its own interests and excludes outsiders. The domestic political situation of a country and its international relationships with other countries are specific examples. The avarice of a dictator and the mass movement of their arrogant nation with a strong power not only destroy other countries but ruin their country itself. Adolf Hitler and the Nazis make supreme examples, but we know that there have been innumerable wars that have erupted under totalitarian regimes. Ranging from small troubles to war, humans are far crueler than other creatures. For example, strong beasts like tigers do not intentionally kill others of the same species. They hunt animals of other species to feed their cubs and themselves. Humans, out of greed, engage in wars to occupy other countries and exploit them.

Is there not a common source of the individual problem of agony and international conflict? We find no fundamental difference between the two. The common cause of all conflicts is the egoic mind, the person or group's sense of self-importance. But the ego is the false self that thinks without a fully calm, pure awareness of the environment as it is. The ego distinguishes itself as the subject from others as objects in thinking and feeling. It is the false self that confronts the world outside, trying to manipulate the objects in a self-centered way. More strictly speaking, it is the force that keeps us in the madness.

Religion must be a major way of saving people from this madness of the ego. In addition, many of them hold on to the theological doctrines and dogmas of their own religion while condemning or disregarding the views of other religions. Egoistic individuals, sometimes knowingly and sometimes unknowingly, try to appear to others as if they were living pious lives relying upon the precepts in the Bible or Sutras. This issue of happiness is surely not restricted to matters of being individual. Very conservative believers of a religion tend to practice love and compassion only within their religious community. When faced with the obligation of practicing love and compassion toward people outside of their religious circle, they try to convert the outsiders to their own religion for the sake of the outsiders' spiritual salvation.

Such tenacity, when it grows to be extraordinary, often brings about war, as history tells us. To them, God is the idea that they place on top of their system, as the supreme being outside of their minds. If you are interested in the teachings of contemporary spiritual leaders, you will know that just the most common point that almost all of them, at least apparently, share is that the *true God* is not any abstract idea but the *true nature of the human self* that occupies the center (or the whole) of all individual life and is *universal, cosmic, and infinite*. It is not the concept of *Atman* in Hinduism. In Hinduism, the incorporeal self of an individual is given the name Atman, but I follow the Buddhist way of negating any kind of individual self. What I mean by the true self is infinity itself.

The Buddhist doctrine of *anatman* (Sanskrit; *anatta* in Pali) states that there is no integral and autonomous being of an individual like a "soul." The individual entity is merely an aggregate of the five *skandhas* (elements)— dense form, sensation or emotion, perception, formations, and consciousness— that are always changing according to natural causes and effects. The body and personality of a sentient being are constituted by those components without a separate self that embraces them all. What you call your "self" is actually your "ego," an illusion that you think controls your life.

On the other hand, the ego is the individual self, which is usually called the false self. The ego is some "false" notion of the self that exists abstractly in thought. It must be used as *the means of (phenomenally) representing or manifesting the true self* in a given situation. The oppositions of "right" and "wrong," of "presence" and "absence," do not carry any importance here. First and foremost, the true nature of the human self is not the conditioned self as identified in a given time and space.

In other words, the *true nature* of the ego as an individual self is not the small mind that is characterized by unnecessary anger, jealousy, or hate. However, just taking a glance at human history is enough to prove that humankind, in pursuing happiness, has usually taken the individual ego and the collective ego (the egos of a group or society) as their master. Many wars have been caused by such angry religious people hating other religions that have grown in different cultures and with different creeds. But in fact, if we limit our discussion to major religions—Christianity, Buddhism, Hinduism, or Islam—, we would find the same nature of loving the ultimate reality, which is not reachable with our power of reason and emotion, and of loving others. This matter of pursuing egoistic gratification through religion causes the great majority of social problems, instead of just promoting and maintaining people's belief in the all-embracing truth and their devotion to creating a more peaceful world. Of course, it is beyond question that all these major religions have the same purpose of leading believers to attain the ultimate reality that transcends the nature of the ego.

Are we meant to seek the ways we can find relief from our anger, anxiety, and stress by trying to benefit from others, by loving people inside our own circle, and by looking down upon, excluding, or hating outsiders? Can we reduce life's troubles and find solutions in this way? The truth is that hatred only increases hatred, disputes, conflicts, and war. Are we not expected to seek peace and happiness through reducing conflicts and struggles by first releasing our anxiety, fear, and anger and by keeping our composure? Ordinary people usually do not try to calm down or stop their prejudice and hatred in order to know what is really there behind all they respond and react to. People simply feel an urgency to respond and react to objects that they think are "outside" themselves. When they have no object to hurry to react to, they feel bored. This is because, to them, getting out of the whirlpool of the excitement would mean being motivated by naiveté or strictly conservative religious faith.

A wonderful way of keeping our mind away from distress and anxiety and staying in equilibrium is practicing meditation. I do not propose that you should spend a long time doing this every day. However, I am sure that at least practicing formal or informal meditation would lead you to keep yourself in a peaceful state of mind even when you are in a situation that is stressful or unfavorable. Informal meditation can not only be in the seated/sitting position, but also when walking, eating, and the like. On the first kind of meditation, it seems to me that "seated meditation" was the general term in the past, but "sitting meditation" is more widely favored today, and thus I would like to employ the latter in this book. By practicing meditation in any form, you try to stop disturbing thoughts and recover stability and peace.

Before you start your car, before you attend a meeting with your colleagues, when you feel you are angry with your client, customer, or your family member, or before you start your daily routine or especially work that needs strong concentration, I recommend you give yourself a moment to take at least a few breaths—deep breathing is OK, but it does not have to be deep breathing. Just try to slow down your normal breathing. If you reach the point of having slow breathing, you will find yourself composed and feel confident in handling the stressful situation. Then, as you work with that effect, you will surely come to expect reliable effects from meditating on a daily business. It is OK to tell others to reduce their anger or nervousness by practicing meditation, but you should be a successful example of a person with a composed state of mind. You can then find a point where they will agree with you and share peace.

Most people who have succeeded in overcoming one or two disturbing situations may think that would suffice. They think they are too busy to try more than that. One of the main reasons not to meditate is always being "busy." But actually, if you want to have more psychological and spiritual power to prevent agitation and disrupted situations or handle them with more equanimity, you need to build a habit of regularly practicing sitting meditation without moving around and staying composed.

When it comes to Buddhist meditation or Christian contemplative/ centering/breath prayer, it is mainly sitting meditation or prayer with almost no words. Spending some time doing sitting meditation definitely brings you the great effect of staying in a peaceful mind. Studies show the excellent effects of meditation—memory improvement, having insight into work and life, efficiency enhancement, as well as dealing with difficult situations with calmness. Then, reading literary masterpieces and watching great films in the way I will introduce later will also guide you to enter a new state of mind and spirituality.

However, if you are not used to being in a meditative state of mind, or if you consider yourself a beginner, you may not easily come to have a mind to start meditation. Neither sitting and walking meditation nor trying to remain staying in that state of mind throughout your daily life would attract your attention. You may not easily find any meditation practitioner among your family members, colleagues, or friends who can introduce you to the depth of meditation. You may just want to follow what interests you, thinking that the best way of living is seeking happiness, judging between right and wrong. Even though you know your interests change swiftly and that you hear meditation works for stress reduction, health improvement, and acquiring the power of profound wisdom, you just would not go on to practice it enough to have such effects. It might still seem odd to you. Or it is possible that when you first attempt meditation, you fall asleep and become reluctant to start again.

If you want to taste meditation more, I would recommend that you begin by simply breathing a few times before starting your car or at your desk before work. Meditation is right for you—where you are now. By meditation I do not only mean sitting meditation. Walking meditation and keeping still and fully awake throughout everyday life will bring inner peace and deeper insight into what you do. Or you can just watch some YouTube videos on Vipassana/mindfulness meditation or Zen and attend a weekly meditation group meeting once or twice to motivate yourself. Some people know Zen as a Japanese tradition in Mahayana Buddhism, but it is also the most popular name for the same Buddhist tradition in other Northern Asian countries—Ch'an in Chinese, Seon in Korean, and Tien in Vietnamese.

Q: Nowadays, countless people throughout the whole world, including 15% of the United States' population, meditate and very much favor and try to follow Buddha's teachings. What new issues can meditation make us aware of?

In this opening chapter, I would like to lay down a general and brief view of the spirituality of the human self that is now known to the public who are interested in this field, at least to some degree. I present what is shared by religious leaders, especially Buddhist, Christian, and secular spiritual leaders, from my perspective, nourished on the ground of my academic achievements and my spiritual experience. This is the first step of our inquiry into the way of improving the spiritual condition of humanity, especially in relation to literature and film.

I know there are innumerable people who have been meditating in America and others who learn from spiritual teachers who have been training as religious people, especially Buddhists. This book will help those who want to live without much stress or even wish to be awakened from the dreamlike life. By this, I mean life itself, just like everything that takes place in a dream, has no fixed, stable laws or principles, and this fact confuses those who are not spiritually awakened. That is, the ego as the false self does not willingly accept the hard necessity for the destruction of its construct. The intensity of the ego consistently creates a prison.

Particularly for the sake of those who have not had a chance to meditate or who are not interested in such an activity of quietly observing the inner world, let us go back to the main issue of this beginning chapter. I would like to reaffirm that prior to being able to discuss anything else, including meditation through literature and film, the point of departure would have to be like the following question: "Why do we ever need to calm down and be composed?" This has to be the question to be put above all else, since "calming down" and staying in a state of composure or equanimity is necessary for all meditation practitioners.

The purpose of meditation is first to relax and be composed, precisely because when you are composed and not in a state of being attached to the forms of outside objects and confused, you become able to find and recover your true self. Then you would have the capacity to perform your work better than when you do without meditating. You would find yourself handling your work with more wisdom, deeper insights, and loving kindness. This is because your true self is not limited to what you do but comprises everything. It is the source of suffering and distress as well as that of loving kindness. Your true self is not limited to you, so I would like to call it "the" true self, not "your" true self. The true self is not your separate, individual self but the whole self.

If we practice meditation on a daily basis and try to keep the meditative mind all day every day, we would experience genuine joy and bliss which transcends superficial feelings of happiness that has its other side—sadness or unhappiness (as will be explained in the next part). We would attain a lasting peaceful state without the tenacious strength of the ego. The benefits have been studied and reported on numerous occasions. According to these studies, meditation would give you a variety of neurological, psychological, and even physical advantages. In this new era, the early part of the 21st century, it has been reported by reliable sources that a large number of Americans practice meditation. Yes, according to different studies, at present, around 15% of the American adult population practice Buddhist (Vipassana/mindfulness and/or Ch'an/Seon/Zen) meditation.[2] The number would be greater if the practitioners of Christian contemplative/centering prayer were included.

Of course, there are many different types of meditation, depending on religious sects and also on large groups that follow non-religious/secular spiritual leaders. The most famous contemporary religious figures who are involved in Buddhist meditation or Christian contemplative prayer are the Reverend Thich Nhat Hanh (1926-), the Dalai Lama (1935-), Fr. Thomas Merton (1915-68), Fr. Thomas Keating (1923-2018), and Fr. Richard Rohr (1943-), just to name a few. The most prominent secular spiritual leaders are Alan Watts (1915-73), Eckhart Tolle (1948-), Ram Dass (1931-2019), Ken Wilber (1949-), and Adyashanti (1962-), among others. All of them, without exception, teach us to try our best to decrease the unnecessary, intense power of ego and to eventually attain the breakthrough to spiritual awakening.

For my part, studying the thoughts of Buddhism and Taoism, and especially Western philosophies and literature, and inspired by those open-minded religious and secular spiritual leaders mentioned above, I would like to present how their thoughts and experience would work for literary reading and film watching. I would like to introduce the heart of my view as "postmodern ethics," which is "a new system of ideas to contribute to the ethical development of literature and the arts of the new age"[3] (I see "postmodern ethics" in a

---

[2] Meditation has become one of the most powerful and effective trends in the U.S. to make life healthy and fulfilling. In 2017, 14.2% of American adults said that they had meditated "within the past year, a threefold increase from 4.1% in 2012, according to a report from the CDC" (Angelica LaVito, "More Americans are meditating than ever before, as mindfulness goes mainstream," *CNBC*, November 8, 2018, https://headtopics.com/us/more-americans-are-meditating-than-ever-before-as-mindfulness-goes-mainstream-2397486). It is also reported that 40% of Americans in religious groups meditate frequently—"at least weekly" (David Masci and Conrad Hackett, "Meditation is common across many religious groups in the U.S.," *Pew Research Center*, January 2, 2018, https://www.pewresearch.org/fact-tank/2018/01/02/meditation-is-common-across-many-religious-groups-in-the-u-s/). Noticeably, "16% of people in the age group 45 to 64 years old practice meditation" and "women are more likely to practice meditation" (Arthur Zuckerman, "46 Meditation Statistics: 2019/2020 Benefits, Market Value & Trends," *CompareCamp.com*, May 22, 2020, https://comparecamp.com/meditation-statistics/). It is also reported in the same article that more and more schools have meditation programs in their curricula And that "[a]lmost 10 times more children have practiced meditation since 2012."

[3] Jae-seong Lee, *Postmodern Ethics, Emptiness, and Literature: Encounters between East and West* (Lanham: Lexington Books, 2015), 19.

different sense to Zygmunt Bauman). I am certain that the meaning of "postmodern ethics" can be understood by *the public*. What worth would it have if people did not understand the experts' esoteric ideas? I would like to link the spiritual inspiration I have attained from these open-minded theologians and spiritual leaders with the academic thoughts of postmodernists and, going further, with Eastern thoughts of Buddhism and Taoism.

At this point, I would like to briefly introduce the basic feature of postmodern ethics to the general audience. "Deconstruction" is a way of freeing the duality of metaphysics from its structure and nature of dualism. It became a well-known term in English literature due to Jacques Derrida (1930-2004), who contributed greatly to the work of freeing Western thoughts from the shell of dualism. Derrida was most influenced by Edmund Husserl (1859-1938), Martin Heidegger (1889-1976), and Emmanuel Levinas (1906-95), who criticized Western metaphysics' inherent nature of dualism and developed it in their own ways. Levinas, who is the main figure of my study, pointed out that the nature of the whole of Western metaphysics is "ontology," a study of existence whose nature is essentially dual (being and non-being). His postmodern/poststructural philosophy is specifically called "ethics." Broadly speaking, postmodern ethics includes Derrida, Jacques Lacan (1901-81), Jean-François Lyotard (1924-98), Gilles Deleuze (1925-95), and others.

However, it seems to me that contemporary Western postmodern ethics does not carry the importance of spirituality. I am convinced that postmodern ethics should be combined with the Mahayana Buddhist view of the ultimate reality. Thus, I have two purposes in producing this book. Firstly, I unite intellectuality and spirituality, handling various fields together— philosophical intellectuality, both religious and secular, and literature and film—in an interdisciplinary way. My second purpose is to communicate with the general public so that they easily share these precious ideas. Having learned all these thoughts, I was always full of desire to learn more. Nevertheless, I am now sure that I am eager to share my ideas with a wider audience. I truly wish to help the general public to better understand literature, film, and other art forms.

In the 21st century, whether you like it or not, we are living in the era of *post*modernism. Postmodernism as a mode of thinking and living arose across philosophy and criticism of literature, the arts, architecture, etc. in the mid to late 20th century after humankind had experienced World War II, which proved the terrible faculty of modernism. Modernism was the big issue that described the whirlpool of efforts to educate, enlighten (edify), and develop the intellectuality of people. The negative side of modernism was the nature of tyranny and violence.

To unite Eastern and Western thoughts for the purpose of having a whole view of human thought in the light of the ultimate Truth, or the genuine liberty of humanity, I would first like to discuss the generally acknowledged fact that Western thought has been assured to innately have *dualism*. Western philosophy is now prevalent around the world of today, and this means that general human thinking in this age is basically in the form of duality. Traditional Western philosophy and theology have had *supreme reason* as their prime object. But I would highlight the change in Western people's thought. The postmodern Western thought of today also shows that it would see its own purpose far more clearly with the help of Eastern thought. My discussion goes on with my conviction that the primary problem with the Western mode of thinking is on the grounds of "dualism," which is in the structure of "binary opposition." For both scholars and general readers, *binary opposition* is the form with which to understand this problem of conflicts arising from reason and rationality.

In Western thought, which is largely said to have begun with Plato and Aristotle, reason and rationality were always considered to be higher than emotion, but in fact, those faculties worked to tie the polar opposites that construct a finite, narrow egoic thought. It is now a common sense that this is the innate weakness of Western metaphysics.

I have elaborated on binary opposition in great detail through the whole of my previous work, *Postmodern Ethics, Emptiness, and Literature: Encounters between East and West,* with reference to both Eastern and Western philosophies. In the present book, I lay emphasis on binary opposition not only as the structure of thinking or as the ego construct, but as the basis for transcending itself. Then I explain how "postmodern ethics," the ethical and theological aspect (pursuing genuine transcendence) of postmodernism, does this work of self-transcending in pursuing non-duality. After all of this history, what is still needed is not the thinking capacity for acute reasoning but the opposite, the unknowable. In contemporary literary criticism, the unknowable is pursuable with "affect" that lies beyond reason and emotion. We need to know more about affect. Our discussion in this chapter will reach the point of the need for the *affect theory* as a synthesizing view of what is being explored in this new era. Then the next chapter will be focused on the solution to dualism from the perspective of the affect theory.

Q: All these spiritual leaders have one common issue, although their views of humanity and the world vary. Whatever style of meditation they contend, they all agree that the ego has to be abolished. If we abandon the ego, will we not lose the power of thinking and our grip of consciousness? How can we live on without perception? Is their view not nihilistic or pessimistic?

The issue of spiritual awakening must not be misunderstood in a nihilistic or pessimistic sense and dismissed. It means that you enter the dimension of the secret and enigmatic movement of *perfect emptiness,* or *Emptiness,* as I always write it with the purpose of signifying it as the depictive name for the ultimate reality or truth. Yes, it is true that Emptiness is a name that reveals the nature of the exterior of our thinking and feeling. It is the dimension of the fundamental power of living with pure joy and bliss, without the oscillation between transitory pleasures and suffering from anxieties. You come to live a life in a lasting state of inner peace, genuine joy, and true insight into life only when you abandon your egoic desire for self-satisfaction with materials and sensuousness. The egoic desire is satisfied with the shallow feelings of pleasure and happiness, and it does not meet your pure desire to encounter the true self. Only the true self leads you to live with fundamental wisdom.

It is also critical to be keenly aware that the ego is the thinking self, and thus that without the ego, we are not able to perceive, understand, or judge phenomena and others' ideas as right or wrong. The pure awareness that is perfectly empty of thought needs the thinking self, although thinking is actually an illusion-making mechanism. Therefore, uniting the two opposite sides, pure awareness and the thinking ego, I propose that thinking and judgment should be done with the power of the *minimal phenomenality* of the ego, which is *the smallest amount of selfhood.* In Buddhist terms, minimum selfhood belongs to the Middle Path between the polar opposites— the beginning point where thinking starts. It does not take sides phenomenally but beyond phenomenality; it both embraces and denies both sides. Thus, judgment should be made where pure awareness and practical egoic power meet. For example, the best judgment is made and the best inner peace is gained at the point where both happiness and pains are embraced, and one side has a more powerful grip.

Otherwise, the *unnecessary, intense power of ego* (which I call *ego intensity*) arises in the form of too much happiness, self-admiration, superiority, anger, jealousy, hatred, and violence that are the sources of racism, sexism, dictatorship, nationalism, and international war. When the *ego intensity* fails to harm others, it turns against itself and comes to have impulses of stress, pain, inferiority, shame, self-hate, cowardice, fear, and even death. You may easily find that when the power of your shallow self, the ego, strengthens, it becomes very capricious and lays judgment on an outside object or on you first as pleasurable, favorable, and strong, and then, in a different situation, as offensive, despicable, cowardly, and hateful. The ego lives on by becoming pleased with the result of its job—comparing and contrasting the images of itself with others. In that sense, the ego is so fanciful that it is like a chimpanzee in a jungle that swings from tree to tree using its arms. It simply sees things outside its own realm, and itself too, only as objects, and does not confront the purest, real dimension of itself.

Let me elucidate this connection more. The intensity of just the raw sense of the egoic judgment is always fundamentally outside the source of true happiness or bliss. Living with an ego intensity indicates the state of human living outside of Paradise as a result of God's punishment for eating the fruit of the tree of knowledge of good and evil, as is expressed in a symbolic way in the Book of Genesis in the Old Testament. In Paradise, Adam and Eve had the power of the *minimal phenomenality* of the ego as the faculty of perceiving objects. The minimal phenomenality of the ego is the basis for positive conceptualization/reasoning and decision-making. It means that you are not attached to your ego, which seems to serve you positively but really confines you in a prison-like narrow mind.

What is usually called "ego" is ego intensity, as I name it here. Ego intensity raises thinking—conceptualization by comparing and contrasting its condition and others'. Of course, conceptualization goes together with emotions—pleasure and pain, happiness and suffering, and excessive pride and fear/cowardice. Without the intensity of ego, you will have more wisdom from pure consciousness. If you do not have the unneeded surplus of the ego's power, your minimal amount of thinking capacity manifests the pure, universal, infinite consciousness and does the right reasoning and makes decisions correctly. You will actually be wiser to manage your daily life affairs. In short, you are not in prison. If you identify yourself with your egoic power too much, you ARE the prison! Since you are not attached to the ego, you still can make a judgment on the grounds of Emptiness, the pure awareness without the ego intensity. It means that you are in a position to make the smartest decision in the situation in which you are placed.

Calming down and maintaining composure is the first step into spiritual depth and obtaining true wisdom and enlightenment. That is why practicing meditation in stillness remains a vital and necessary part of Buddhism. Contemplative centering/silent/meditative prayer has been part of the traditions of Catholicism, the Eastern Orthodox Church, and Quakerism (a Protestant sect). In fact, only when your mind calms down and stays composed and equanimous can you realize what is truly going on in the heart of your life. It has been proven in cognitive science, and even some quantum physicists have proved that we can benefit from meditating, and some try to combine science and meditation. Now, that is the practical purpose of meditation and staying in a meditative state of mind. Thus, you do not want to have the image of an ascetic practitioner in the Himalayas in your mind. The first purpose of practicing meditation and trying to be in a meditative state of mind is to improve your life.

1.2. The true nature of the self and the ego

Q: I think I have your point straight. But could you elaborate more on how the true self, or the true sense of God, and ego as the false self are different?

The prime purpose of practicing meditation and staying composed is to reach far beyond those benefits and attain spiritual enlightenment. Meditating and maintaining inner peace in your everyday life would replace your ego, an individual and superficial self with its intractable and unceasing desires, with the true, unlimited self. We always have to try to *calm the ego that is necessarily formed in the growing process down to the original, all-embracing, and infinite true self.* In this sense, the two selves are completely different in nature. The ego is a petty mimicry of the infinite self, whereas the true self is infinity itself beyond time and space.

The true self is the source or origin that forms the individual or separate ego. The true self is Emptiness, or the perfect emptiness with wondrous movement in the Buddhist sense. No wonder it is God in the Christian sense, since it is the dimension of the most fundamental *love*. In this sphere of true love, you are able to see others and the world as such—without attachment to them and beings of a transient nature—or "things-in-themselves," in the words of Immanuel Kant, one of the greatest Western philosophers. By "things-in-themselves," Kant does not mean that we have to admit the different qualities of separate objects like different personalities. Instead, Kant means that all beings and things have the same nature.

Kant observed that there is only one true nature, which is called "Emptiness" in Buddhism. You may find that common nature, Emptiness ("body without organs," in Gilles Deleuze's words), only as your mind becomes empty of its separate nature, the ego. In Buddhism, the true self is metaphorically expressed as a clean, bright mirror. This mirror reflects everything without being disturbed by anything. Just like that mirror, you can see through to the serene depth of life without egoic thoughts. That is, it is none other than your pure nature that is empty of the phenomenal intensity of the ego. In fact, if you truly experience the oneness of your original nature and the original nature of all other humans, other creatures, and inanimate things, it means you are coming closer to the spiritual breakthrough to awakening from the illusory life of suffering.

Fully enlightened ones like Shakyamuni Buddha do not become attached to the presence or the absence (the other form of presence) of outside objects and become anxious. However, one who has awakened from the dreamlike nature of thinking and living is not like a stone statue. Without ego intensity, an enlightened one, or a Buddha, is living every day, every second of life with genuine and unswerving wisdom. Such a person has a free spirit. Liberty here means they are free to think and act on the grounds of true nature. When they concentrate on some work or objects outside themselves, their mind is not attached to objects or get excited or depressed. In other words, awakened beings know that they are in the dream where everything is just unstable and empty of fixity. Buddhas have a clear, free mind to choose between good and evil, right and wrong, beautiful and ugly, but they have lost the intensity or strength of the power of egoic adhesion.

Yet again, real freedom means you are free from the ego intensity that puts you in a prison built by your own discerning mind. If you choose what simply sensuously looks good to you or arouses your fantasy, it would put you in a deadlock or at least in a complex situation. It is possible that in such a situation, you might think you are doing very well by releasing your nervous tension, but that is what your ego does.

Yes, it is a harsh fact that nobody can tell you when to stop delusory thinking. You just have to try to follow what your natural, true mind tells you and reject the egoic desire. The more you are driven to the whirlpool of the complexity of the situation you are placed in, the less peace you will find. Awakened individuals actually have no barrier of the mind; their mind is one with all other beings and phenomena and has no resistance based on egoic desire.

Q: So, true freedom lies beyond the ordinary feelings of happiness and suffering. To employ the story of the first humans in Genesis, the first book of the Old Testament, does it mean we are not genuinely or deeply happy as Adam and Eve were before they were expelled from Paradise?

That is a great question for the sake of a Western audience because Western civilization is based on Christianity. My discussion would be characterized as one that links Eastern and Western *philosophical* thoughts in view of *spirituality* that transcends the ordinary ways of thinking and emotion. As we are staying on the ground of the studies in philosophy and religion that have been serious about humanity and true transcendence for two to three thousand years, we can be safe from the enticement of wrong meditation styles and cults or superstitions. Meditation, not practiced in a strange way, is nothing mystical. In fact, all of the traditional authentic Western philosophers such as Descartes, Kant, Hegel, and Heidegger, just to name a few, have explored the purest state of spirit or mind, characterizing it as infinite, universal, absolute, and true.

The story of the first humans, Adam and Eve, tells us that they were punished by God because they ate the fruit of the tree of the knowledge of good and evil and came to have the intellectual ability to distinguish between good and evil. I propose that this story metaphorically explains that the human subjects began to have the egoic nature and the ability to compare and contrast because they broke the relationship with the absolute truth. As a result of gaining reasoning faculties, humans began to experience anxiety, fear, anger, jealousy, superiority, and inferiority. The ego that resulted from a guilty conscience is the barrier to liberty.

That is to say, before they ate the forbidden fruit, Adam and Eve already had the proper amount of spiritual capacity they needed to live on. They were able to listen to the omniscient and omnipresent God and revere him, but by eating the fruit of the tree of knowledge, they gained an excessive amount of discerning ability that is the power of what we call the ego. The story of the first humans presents to us that we have an amount of capability that we are not able to control. The ego intensity is the vanity of the self, the surplus of capacity we need to distinguish between good and evil. Because of the unnecessary capacity we have, or as a result of Adam and Eve's sin as told in the Biblical story that is an allegory of human nature, we struggle with ourselves when we face unexpected or stressful situations.

From this story, I deduce the following point in view of the future cooperation of Eastern and Western styles of thought. It is positive and significant that Western thinkers have sought truth on the grounds of logic, the human science of objective reasoning, for which comparing and contrasting is necessary. However, what is more important from the perspective of Mahayana Buddhism (in China, Korea, Japan, Vietnam, and Tibet), the abolishment of the ego and the awakening of "the true self" or "the real I" cannot be done on the basis of logic and reasoning. Buddhism always declares that intellectuality and spirituality are radically different.

By eating the fruit of the tree of knowledge of good and evil, humans lost the ability to stay in peace constantly. Yet, in the Buddhist sense, paradise metaphorically expresses the original state of our mind. Our innermost mind is *the awakened state*. Exactly in that sense, we are still in paradise, just like Adam and Eve were before they were punished by being expelled from Paradise, as described in the Book of Genesis, the beginning of the Judeo-Christian Bible. We have not really lost such a genuinely pure, unadulterated mind. As children grow up to be members of society, they come to believe that they have to lose their purity and be bright to fit the role. In other words, they are *deluded* into the idea that they lost their purity to follow God. However, their true nature is always there in their spiritual dimension, which is prior to their intellectuality.

By spirituality, I do not mean the nature of the soul as an incorporeal entity that is believed to outlive physical life. What I mean by spirituality is the quality of pure consciousness beyond the duality formed by such opposites as right and wrong, subject and object, even pure and impure. Spirituality forms our intelligence as the capability for discerning and reasoning. Yet most people do not care about its importance. The issue of spirituality is usually dismissed as too abstract and impractical to consider for living one's daily life. When people try to understand the meanings and values of spirituality, they think about some set of moral laws. Moral laws are not from the innermost part of human life. Moral laws, which consist of the language of principles and precepts set in the social tradition, are in a dual form.

Q: If I surrender to God in me, or the ultimate reality, would I be rewarded?

Without any possibility of doubt, there *is* a reward for surrender. Being truly spiritual, one's mind attains genuine wisdom coming out of its fountain that lies beyond the appearances of phenomena. You come to dwell within the well of wisdom without being consciously aware of it. First and foremost, you will have the wisdom to know that the true fountain of life, and thus the only true source of wisdom, is spirituality. Then one becomes able to deal with various things in life with that wisdom, facing difficulties and having relationships with others with love, compassion, and even more logical reasoning. In any event, the ego, your individual or separate self, has to give way to the universal, infinite self. It never means that the thinking capacity of your brain decreases and you become like a dummy, puppet, or scarecrow. The form of the ego remains the supporter of the true self, the lively, moving Emptiness.

The point is that if we lay our ego down and enter the space of true peace and just positively accept what the universe/world/life is, we surely have the precious spiritual feeling beyond ordinary emotion, the real sense of calm bliss, joy, and infinity, and we can carry that peace in all the activities that we do in daily life. The Book of Revelation (7:17, 21:6, and 22:1) and the Gospel of John (4:14 and 7:37) in the New Testament as well as many parts of the Psalms show us that the tree of life and the water of life are provided for us. Surely, the water of life in these examples means the Holy Spirit. No doubt, these parts of the Bible are a witness of *our truly spiritual and infinite life*. We do have absolutely the right judgment and really eternal life, but this is all covered by our unnatural capacity of egoic knowledge and judgment with that false knowledge.

The core of our intellectuality is empty of the egoic nature, since our intellectuality is a tool for the universal self, which is God in terms of identity. The excessive amount of thinking capability reflects that we have the nature of self-denial that creates duality. Duality created Taoism, in which the two sides are expected to supplement each other. Taoism stems from Lao-zi and Chuang-zi, who taught in Shakyamuni's age. Jacques Derrida, one of the most prominent postmodern thinkers, also declares the same kind of issue. Yet in actuality, duality causes conflict between the polar opposites—the subject and the outside object, one side of the subject and the other of the subject itself. The human mind and society are always unstable. In this way, anger, sadness, anxiety, jealousy, stress, and even happiness are the appearances of our egoic nature. The negative nature of intellectuality is human folly, which is detrimental to itself. For example, when you get angry, it is you who is first consumed by the burning anger. A war brings another war.

There is another point I would like to bring up. Adam and Eve did not eat the fruit of the tree of life that was in the midst of Eden with the tree of knowledge (Gen. 2:22). I propose it means that while we humans have extreme difficulty with recovering the capability of having real peace of mind, because of the false knowledge produced by egoic thinking and its results, false reasoning and improper emotions like anger, jealousy, one-sided love, happiness as opposed to unhappiness and suffering, we are unaware of the fact that we are also much closer to the awareness that our life is not transitory but in the ultimate reality eternal, even though at first it seems like we are prevented from reaching the tree of life, as the Book of Genesis says (2:24). The beginning of Chapter 22 of the Book of Revelation in the New Testament shows us that the tree of life and the water of life are provided for us. This means that as we attain spiritual enlightenment, we come to know that our true nature is infinite. As is well known in Buddhism, we were not born, and thus we will not die.

I would like to make myself clear that the tree of life, the water of life, and even the tree of the genuine knowledge of real good and evil are right in the grounds of our present moment, and thus are to be found in the present moment itself. The real point is that we must go beyond the ego that depends on the persistence of past-life memories, old habits, and future expectations. The ego is a strong and tenacious construct whose structure is binary opposition, what really pollutes our spirituality, which is never separate from the highest judgment, eternal life, and genuine wisdom of what we do in our daily lives.

When a baby is born, it is in the ultimate reality without conscious desire that comes from the ego. As the baby grows up, it seems to lose this paradise as it comes to have the ego intensity, a defense mechanism against others. Later in life, s/he can be motivated by various experiences to realize their true self. Important activities that can offer us such moments to encounter the true self are reading literary works, watching films, practicing meditation, creating artworks, or simply exercising. These activities lead us to empty our mind of egoic cravings.

In such a way, as you awake from your unconscious dreaming with unhappiness, suffering, and pain, as well as excessive pleasure or shallow happiness, the ego loses its intensity. Thus, an enlightened one has his/her personality without intensity. The ego intensity gives way to the power of infinity, which means that your life is healed and filled with a new energy of animation without depression, grief, or stress. The primary place is now empty of thought or the image of phenomena, and the infinite Emptiness is the very fountain of the living power. Your spirit lives fully in your individual personality and body without wasting time and energy with unnecessary thought. You know that all is in the present moment, that all you have is the here and now. There is only here and now; the here and now never lacks anything, and you clearly know it. More than that would give you the effects of stress on your mind and body.

This spiritual growth is not only a matter for individuals; it is also an issue for the *evolution of humankind*. The changes and movements of the human mind gave birth to the ego, and we are in the middle of a development toward the egoless phase of living. I am convinced that greed, conflict, anxiety, jealousy, anger, and war are illusory but necessary phenomena for us to overcome. From a higher position, the violent, negative side of the ego can provide us with momentum to intensify the enhancement of spirituality. From a higher perspective, violence is serving the ego as it intends to surrender to spirituality by abolishing itself. In this light, humanity as a whole is in progress—from a pre-ego state (ape) through the contemporary species of *Homo sapiens* to a new, egoless, truly loving humankind.

The issues on artificial intelligence (AI) or machine intelligence and cybernetic organisms (cyborgs) are now popular, but I do not want to involve them in terms of spiritual capacity. We are witnessing obvious scientific and technological developments. Machines will increasingly have more intellectual capability, and the threat of AI to society may be serious in various aspects. However, I am unwaveringly convinced that at the end of the day, AI could not possess human spiritual power. As far as humanity is concerned, the new era must be that of spiritually heightened humans. AI is produced by the ego, the human capacity to create in its own images. Everything is allowed in terms of the variations of the true self, and machines with intelligence much higher than ours are included in this. However, it is clear to me that machines will never be able to take the place of the true self, the universal spirit itself, at least not for now.

Q: OK, then how can I know that I am present with the true self/God/Emptiness, which is the origin of my ego (formed in the individual situations of my life)?

Above all, your true self is the source of your ego, and thus your thinking. The fountain of your finite, transient, constantly changing ideas and things is the infinite true self. The transient image of appearances is only the form that the ego has constituted at a certain time and in a certain space. What has happened in the limits of time and space is a variation of the limitless true self. The real self is outside of the false, or ordinary, self. It is not some other dimension than that of the ordinary self of a human who thinks, eats, and works in daily life. As the source of matters and events, the true self is just "empty" of the phenomenal nature of existence.

The true self is neither in the state of a phenomenally moving mind nor in that of an unmoving, stable mind. It is the immaculate flow of perfect emptiness beyond or prior to perception. It does not have any intrinsic existence, and it is perfectly devoid of any illusive thought process. In other words, it is not a mind-generated state at all. The true self is not a selfhood like the ego, and the ego is not able to carry it through language or thought. Ideas and words can never describe *emptiness* in any proper way. As taught in Buddhism, even lying beyond one's personality, the true self is the vast pure consciousness—not only of the individual but of all humans, and also of all animals, plants, and others. It is not limited by any form, while the ego is limited as the form of a local, individual consciousness. The ego is the self of the usual meaning, and the true self is the pure awareness that takes the role of a screen onto which the images of beings, things, phenomena are projected.

Sigmund Freud's theory of psychoanalysis laid too much intensity on the basis of the ego, especially the Oedipus complex (a child's unconscious sexual desire to kill the parent of the same sex and to have the parent of the opposite sex), and the direct way of interpreting human behaviors in terms of sexuality. Jacques Lacan, who interpreted in his linguistic and poststructural view and is now generally agreed to be the most prominent psychoanalyst after Freud, considered the ego as an *illusion*. As is commonly known, Lacan calls what remains, regardless of the changing reality of daily life, "the Real." The Real is the first of the three psychoanalytic orders (registers, divisions) in Lacanian psychoanalytic theory. Like the screen that allows all images on it, the Real is the ultimate source of all individual psychic movements. The Real is the whole, not the individual self. In other words, the Real is the integral, vital spirit. The imaginary and the symbolic as the two psychological orders come into being in a very early stage of a child. The imaginary engenders desires it first feels within the relationship with the mother, and the symbolic expresses it in language and socialization.

To me, it is crucial that these two phases (which almost overlap) are the way of reaching the Real. The relationship with the mother as the object is already the beginning of the separation from the formless Real. As I will elaborate upon in the next chapter, the Real remains wholly *other* than what the ego as the self believes it is. Thus, it is explained by Lacanian psychoanalysis that the ego is a *false* self. The ego is by nature the selfish power that falls short of the true reality. Through "the mirror stage" that Lacan describes as the formation of the ego through the self-objectifying process, a child is alienated from the Real, the true, unutterable self. Nonetheless, as a tool, the ego is not always useless and harmful. Well used without its nature of egoic attachment, it presents to the unmanifested real self a wide variety of possibilities to manifest itself.

Some Lacanians place emphasis on the Real prior to the birth of the ego as what we are alienated from in infancy, but it seems clear to me that finding the real self later in adult life is far more important. As mentioned earlier, sitting/walking meditation, simple activities like running, and efforts to stay in that state of mind throughout your daily life would greatly help you to have the effect of dwelling in the "Transmiddle" zone or (junior) *Samadhi*, the ocean of wisdom. (The notion of *Samadhi* is presented in Chapter Three).

In this way, the ego builds one's own world by distinguishing itself from outer reality, understanding external objects, and controlling one's thoughts and behaviors. The ego, "me," the centered self, produces an exaggerated sense of self-esteem and self-importance. Meditation places us in a peaceful state of mind and effectively reduces the power of the ego. The purpose of practicing meditation is not to gain some transient, superficial happiness; on the contrary, it greatly helps us to calm down toward the point of no ego and presents us with feelings of bliss, true happiness. The ego is contaminated by its greed, which came into being because of its separation from the whole, and thus it is not pure awareness. As an impure thinking mechanism, it lacks the ability to remain still; it constantly moves and changes its place. It is easy for us all to find our minds very unstable. It is very difficult for the ego to stay calm, even just for one moment.

There is no way of consciously knowing the true self and describing it as one does one's personality. Yet I am convinced there is a possibility of describing what it is like to feel it is your true self with such words as bliss, joy, love, compassion, peace, and sublime. Language cannot describe exactly what spirituality is because those words involve the other side of the presence of conventional meanings—senses of apathy and negligence, for instance. Yet those words are usually employed and the meanings shared as people depict the way toward spirituality.

In any sense, however, encountering the true self does not bring the tension of concentration. Rather, it is the state or condition of stress reduction. Tension is defused and you can perform your task in an easier, wiser way and achieve better, even unanticipated results. I do not intend to illustrate the benefits of meditation here because there is an ample amount of material about the benefits we get from meditating. But in any possible case, the spiritual level is the realm definitely beyond the narrow, local, finite world. In other words, it is the dimension of infinity you can glimpse by reading literature or watching films, as I will explain in great detail as we go on.

If you experience that transcendental realm, you will reach beyond the view of calculating the losses and gains that your intellectualization can do. This is the realm where losing is also gaining. This ability is not a faculty of petty conditional reasoning; it is the competence and aptitude to embrace a wide scope of vision of life and events. As we will see in the next chapter, the spiritual dimension is that of "affect" that is beyond emotion as well as reason. Spirituality enables you to see what is outside the narrow world of measuring, calculating, and even personality. In terms of the postmodern ethics of Emmanuel Levinas, it is the space of "the (wholly) other" of what is not me. The "me"-centered mentality obviously cannot reach the space of the other with its capability of thinking and knowing. The space of the other is over and beyond what man-made "meaning" can ever carry.

Of course, it is never easy to let go of the ego's grip and attain the diamond mind. You may have to suffer the difficulties of removing the hard shell of the ego, especially because it transmutes to please you. The ego changes in nature and form to satisfy itself, but it also does so to disappoint you and make you despair. Strangely enough, it lies to the mind itself as if it is just the substance of yourself, your true self. However, the difficulties do not stop there.

The ego covers the Middle Path, which actually embraces the whole, and by doing so, it shows you either positive or negative feelings. It constantly takes pleasure both by pleasing you and by depressing you. It is smart in disguising itself as your true self. Your ego takes time until you acknowledge its nature as your false self. Nevertheless, the form without intensity actually would not have any power to remove the true nature of the self. Emptiness in itself is never phenomenal, and it does not assume a positive or negative nature. It is the Middle and the whole, but it never loses its power. Yet it is important to note that when it has to, it does take either a positive or negative form, and it shows no limits. That is, the ego's decision without intensity is OK! It is not the essence of your self, and you have to acknowledge and accept just that. When the ego loses its intensity, you have to accept it is how the true self appears. You must know the sheer fact that your true self is always there, empty of any emotional state of mind, but also that you can encounter the true self as your ego gives way.

Emptiness as such does not allow itself to be any phenomenon, but, seemingly paradoxically, it can identify itself with an infinite number of different phenomena. However, whenever we are unsure, we think and act with the power coming from the true self; we would have to make sure that we reduce the intensity of (superficial and transient) happy feelings or depression. Again, meditation through literary reading or watching films, as will be explained, would be a great help.

Q: I am intrigued by your ideas of "the Transmiddle" and would like to ask you to elaborate on it in greater detail, employing Buddhist and Christian ideas.

In short, if the ego is an illusion, it means that only the true self is real, and the nature of the true self is Transmiddle. While the ego takes either of the polar opposites, the true self embraces the other and takes both aspects that comprise the whole. To the ultimate, universal self, taking both sides means being and non-being, presence and absence, doing and non-doing. We need to discuss this more. The ultimate truth is spiritually simple (if you deeply experience it) but difficult to understand intellectually.

I decided to coin the term "Transmiddle" because I have seen so many people misunderstand the Middle Path simply as the middle way between opposite sides, like the color gray instead of black or white. The real meaning of the Middle Path is an all-embracing dimension and not the phenomenally middle place between the polar opposites that form the ego. By using the *Transmiddle* Path, I emphasize we can enjoy the bliss of being one with *the dancing light of truth* that chooses black, white, or any other color in the phenomenal world.

Let me elaborate on it in more detail, taking some time to think about *the true self both as the whole and as the real nature of the ego*. First of all, in Buddhism, especially in the Mahayana tradition, it is called the Middle Path. There is a well-known story about Shakyamuni's teachings on the Middle Path. To a meditation practitioner who asked Shakyamuni about meditation, Shakyamuni answered by taking the example of a good sitar player. Shakyamuni taught the meditator that in order to play the sitar well, the player has to tune the strings of the instrument, but not too tightly or too loosely. If the player tunes the instrument too tightly, the strings would come apart, and if the strings are too loose, it would not produce sound. Through this example, Shakyamuni taught his disciple to avoid both extreme asceticism and self-indulgence.

Now, the Middle Path is usually misunderstood simply as being positioned in the middle between the polar opposites and not going to extremes. However, Shakyamuni's teaching of the Middle Path is not limited to that meaning. The principal Mahayana sutras clearly show that the Middle Path actually means the whole of both presence and absence, being and non-being, subject and object, inside and outside, and finitude and infinity. Once it is the whole of the polarity, it is the whole of the universe, because every being and every thing phenomenally takes on either of the two halves. It is not only the whole of a separate entity but of the whole universe and beyond. It is unlimited infinity. Therefore, the Transmiddle Zone can find its form on either side of the two polar opposites. That is to say, right cannot be right without wrong, presence cannot be presence without absence, and both are only phenomena. The Transmiddle nature of the true self lies beyond the concepts of the two. The Transmiddle has no site in phenomena, but it gives rise to both aspects.

Ultimately, there is no real difference between the two. Therefore, it is right to say that the true self as the whole is not only the ultimate but also a unique reality. Put in other words, the infinite number of separate egos is just ontologically/phenomenally different forms of the formless true, universal self. Yet in the *light* of the true self, the always *moving, changing, dancing whole,* it would be foolish to say that the ego is simply negative and valueless. It is Buddha's nature, Christ's consciousness, or the *dancing light* that freely engenders phenomena. Again, the true self is unlike the ego, which is the presence of self-identity. It is not just the presence of a certain ideal mental state, nor is it its absence, because absence is also the concept of an absent "state." The forms seem to us so real, but in reality, the nature of the appearances is illusory.

Our nature is Emptiness without an egoic desire for possession. Emptiness in the Buddhist sense is perfect stillness with wondrous movement. It is not a state of movement, nor does it belong to that of the stability of the condition of a non-moving state of absence or nothingness. It is the unconditional beyond time and space. This is what I would like to call the "Transmiddle Path." The Transmiddle Path, or Zone, is true Emptiness, and true Emptiness is our true self—*unconditional love*. That is, in ultimate reality, there is only true nature, the Transmiddle, and it finds its form in a given situation by taking either of the two halves of the binary opposites that constitute a phenomenon, of which I have given examples above.

The true self is prior to the beginning of all phenomena. It would never appear in a concrete form such as an idea or desire to obtain a visible being, thing, or any tangible result. Yet the real I is the true nature of the conditioned individual self, ego, and the ego is the separate form of the true I. That is why the *Heart Sutra,* one of the representative sutras in Mahayana Buddhism, says: "Emptiness is form, form is emptiness." Beyond doubt, it does not mean that the true self is just the outward, transient form in itself. You have to use your thinking ego in a healthy, positive way, but at the end of the day, there is only one nature which embraces both sides and does not cling to either—the Transmiddle Zone.

From your everyday life experiences, you might want to say that living your life just in itself is so precious and not illusory. Well, yes! Life is priceless, and so are you! "Illusion" here is not to be understood in a negative sense. Rather, it means that everything changes and nothing lasts in a stable state. In Buddhist terms, every being, every thing, and every phenomenon is *impermanent.* Moreover, you cannot really expect that affairs will go as you want. A great success may offer you joy today, but it could turn out to be not such a wonderful success later. Or if you find someone has achieved a much greater success, it is possible that you would be enveloped in flames of jealousy. In contrast, a dreadful deadlock could take a very positive turn tomorrow. This is the dream quality of life that lets us say life is illusory. It seems to me perfectly evident that no one can deny it. However, people are stuck to their desire to have "more"—more money, more fame, more good looks, sex with more people, etc.—that only offer them fleeting values, and they are not interested in what they will encounter if they let go of their desire. The egoic desire goes against itself and eventually destroys itself like Jekyll against Hyde. Jekyll's killing of Hyde results in nothing but suicide, as I will elaborate in Chapter Five.

Hence, instead of just following your desire, wherever it seems to go, if you look into that desire and become aware of its impermanent nature, you would know the sheer fact that there is actually only emptiness. From emptiness, which is the true self, everything comes into life and disappears. It is correct to say that the true, unconditioned, unlimited self is the same as the infinite universe. As long as your mind is not attached to transient appearances, you would feel that you and the world outside are one. Or, to put it in other words, you would feel that the world outside is a diluted version of your inner self. Your true self is the dreamer of your life as a dream, so to speak. The real you is the one who dreams.

Whatever the content of the dream may be, the elements and meaning are made up by the ego, the original identity of which is the true self, but the real dreamer is the true self. The ego is just the ground where the real self plays. The dreamer, the one who is dreaming, is your true, unlimited self, so you can say that everything is possible, and in the ultimate reality, the seemingly polar opposites—good and evil, right and wrong, love and hatred, high and low—are equal. The true self is the real love that embraces both. Jesus' saying "Love your enemy" demonstrates the nature of the true self.

Again, the dreamer, the unlimited self, dreams through your conditioned ego, which distinguishes between good and evil in the given situation. Good and bad are determined by your conditioned ego, the real nature of which is the true self. Therefore, ultimately, good and bad are the result of the condition that your ego judges as bad. You always have to remind yourself that there are possibilities of being conditioned and having a result in other ways than the one you choose. The true nature of yourself is the real nature of every thing, every being, and all of the world and universe, and your ego, the conditioned mimicry of the true self, misunderstands the law of "interdependent co-arising."

Your true nature is not *yours* only. As the ultimate reality, it is the reality of everyone, everything, and every phenomenon. It is the reality of the world; it is the reality of the universe. It is that which produces the ultimate reality of all phenomena. There is not even one phenomenon, being, or thing that does not belong to the true substance. Everything is interconnected with everything else. Everything in the universe is interconnected beyond the limits of the phenomenal. The true reality of all is purity beyond the concepts of purity and impurity. Purity perceived as pure is not truly pure; it is a mere concept of being pure as opposed to being impure. The ultimate reality means all existences are one.

That all are one beyond limits indicates unconditional love, not the feeling of attachment identified as love. All individuals are one in ultimate reality, and you as an individual can offer unconditional love for others in whatever you do every day. In each given situation, for example, whether at work, with your family, or when alone, you can manifest the formless reality, Emptiness, without a self-centered nature.

I know many would disagree with me and say that human nature is not so naïve or pure as to offer everything to others. Well, I cannot but say that they misunderstand human nature and the ultimate reality of the mind. The ultimate reality or love does not mean the state of mind that would offer everything to others. Nor would you have to remind yourself immediately about helping such poor people as orphans, widows, and the homeless. The ultimate reality of the human mind and society is the Transmiddle. You are not obliged to be on either of the opposites that form the binary opposition, for there is no moral rule that you must observe. It may sound ironic that true love is the power that comes from the dimension of pure consciousness that embraces all, not from a burden of moral obligation to live in a certain pattern that you think is ideal. It is good to have a warm heart to help the destitute, but for example, you do not have to feel a burden of moral responsibility or scarify yourself for not helping them whenever you come across them. Such a guilty conscience does not come from truly unconditional love for everyone and everything. True, unconditional love is non-egoistic and non-conceptual awareness. As truly unconditional love embraces all, it includes your individuality (your own individual feelings and thoughts) as its element. Your self-awareness is not limited to being a separate existence.

When Jesus said "Love your neighbor as you love yourself," he did not mean you should ignore your own situation. True love is rather the uncontaminated, uncommitted, calm, wise, and ethical mind to be open to all others, whosoever they are, with the aim that they can help themselves. Yet the Transmiddle Zone is the dimension of perfect liberty, ethical responsibility (yet without a moral set of rules to stick to), and wisdom that is not tempted to either extreme—unreasonable sacrifice or indifference and uninterest. An ethical mind is *never* one of stupidity.

It is clear that being one here is by no means to be used politically. Throughout history, dictators have worked their people hard with the idea of uniting the country. Their political slogans such as "one people, one world" were always used to bind their citizens together under their control with strong political power. International war criminals used such slogans as a tool when they led their armies to invade neighboring countries.

The true self as (pure) "consciousness" or (pure) "awareness" is the most common and greatest point that all secular spiritual leaders including Eckhart Tolle, Wilber, Rupert Spira, Deepak Chopra, and Paulo Coelho share. Christian mystics and Buddhists, particularly Mahayana Buddhists, have held to the same view. Their thoughts are not drawn from solid mathematical, scientific experiments and proof. To be sure, there are some scientists who struggle to demonstrate their views of unified field theory (coined by Albert Einstein) or the theory of everything in such areas as superstring theory, by which they would be able to explain the profound energy and vitality of the subatomic particles and nature from one single theoretical stance. Even the God particle (Higgs boson) has been confirmed to have been discovered. But scientists have not yet reached a conclusion that could be generally agreed upon and shared as the final theory. Nonetheless, the spiritual teachers' perspective on the one universal consciousness is not a new view at all. It has been agreed, shared, and explored by an infinite number of people throughout the long history of philosophy, art, and religion.

Buddhism is the supreme example of the spiritual quest for the ultimate and the plainest truth. For nearly 2,600 years since the time of its founder, Shakyamuni Buddha (c. 5th to 4th century BCE), Buddhism has offered theosophy, religious philosophy, and speculation about the inconceivable nature of spirituality. Buddhist philosophy has provided us with ways in which humans could enter the spiritual dimension that is beyond the ego. The dimension of spirituality or universal consciousness is the exteriority of subjectivity that can exist only in the form of "binary opposition," the dual structure of the ego, the ordinary self (conditioned by concepts gained in the culture) separating itself from other selves and the world outside. The prime teaching of Shakyamuni Buddha is that you should overcome the ego, the illusory self that causes great suffering, and be awakened to the highest enlightened state of mind. In Mahayana Buddhism, the true self is called "Buddha nature," or simply "Buddha." It is the ultimate reality of the universal, true self. According to the earlier analysis, only the structure of the ego should remain. The intensity of the ego has to go.

From the Christian vantage point, one of the examples you would want to take is the example of the vine that Jesus uses to explain that you must be a good branch that bears much fruit, while he is the true vine (John 15:1-5). Jesus' self or spirit is the vine. The vine is *Christ's self,* or God's *Holy Spirit.* When you dwell in Christ's self and Christ's self dwells in you, you think and act right in the true nature. In the Buddhist view, Christ's self or the Holy Spirit is the universal Emptiness, which is the power of creation. Creation has not just been done once and for all, as you might think if you are interested in relating the creation story in the Bible to the Big Bang theory and astronomy. God's creation continues everywhere in the universe, and it is constantly performed through your existence and the existences of other beings. To employ a Hindu term, the universe or world is the stage of God's divine dance of *Lila.* It can also be said that the life of every single one of us forms a creative divine play of God. That is, the true nature of all of us is divine. Boldly but clearly speaking, at the deepest level, our true nature is God.

To take another example, the true self is like a cinema screen or TV screen onto which constantly changing images are projected. These projected images are sometimes pleasurable ones, but we also see sad or terrible images on the screen. Living life, we experience various kinds of situations and conditions—pleasant and delightful or sad and terrible. The changing images on the screen can be similes to the reaction of the ego to the people and the events taking place in certain circumstances. The screen, on the contrary, is not affected by the images projected onto it—whether it is an extremely pleasing situation or an extremely horrifying one, the screen just allows everything on it, yet never is pleased or stressed. As mentioned earlier, the mirror has been used as a notorious metaphor to explain the true self in the Ch'an/Seon/Zen tradition in Mahayana Buddhism since ancient times. A mirror reflects everybody and everything without egoic evaluation and judgment. There is no prejudice or attachment in the process of reflection.

What matters in these examples is that the screen and mirror accept all that happens without discrimination. These objects are symbolic of the all-embracing love that lies beyond the feeling of love as attachment, as opposed to that of hate. This fundamental, ineffable love includes both feelings of love as attached feeling and hate. When a good situation is projected, the screen takes it on itself without reservation, and when a sad or even terrible event takes place, the screen or mirror never objects.

However, it is noticeable that the nature of the true self is not stale and boring. It is the nucleus of life itself with vitality. Those awakened ones would be delighted in a pleasant situation and sorrowful at other's misfortunes, as they are conditioned to be. What is most important, though, is that these people would not lose the keen awareness that they are one with the world. They also have ultimate wisdom and insight into life and what they do. Enlightened people also enjoy the incomparable beauty of life that sentient beings cannot even imagine! They have an unwavering experiential conviction in the true self within. It is perfectly grounded in the pure experience of the true self, not in discerning thoughts. It is never an idea that is formed in connection to past experience and future experience.

The true self as the Transmiddle space, not attached to either side of the opposites, is both beyond and within any phenomenal position. It is simple Emptiness that can be filled with joy, sadness, or whatever kind of sensation, but it is undoubtedly beyond, behind, or beneath brain functions such as perceiving, knowing, reasoning, discerning, judging, decision-making, and memorizing. Those brain functions serve social and habitual standards previously infused in the mind forming the structure of the ego. Spirituality is detached from all brain functions.

The true self is pure consciousness. Consciousness needs to be aware of itself reflected from outside objects, although not in a directly corporeal way. I would like to advance the idea that because pure spirituality takes its form in the thinking egos that make free decisions and their relations with each other, the egos are alright if their intensity to return to themselves is moderated to be in the Transmiddle Zone and do not struggle with themselves and harm others. The ego is the true self in a form, and thus it seems outwardly that the true self allows the ego to take whatever form it needs. Yet those phenomena that cause anxieties and agonies are not really spiritual. There are no unstable set moral laws; ethics is the nature of the true self. True nature comprises forms that can be seen as right or wrong according to different cultures and ages. Only with the power of the ego can you think and judge between good and evil. The fall of the first human beings in the Book of Genesis indicates the birth of the capacity of the egoic judgment at the cost of the loss of their pure awareness and beatitude.

As a manifestation of your true—loving and peacemaking—nature, your ego is meant to be loving and peacemaking as well. Yet egoic love is a feeling of attachment, unless it is widely open to the formless true love and peace. Conversely, your true nature appears as your ego power decreases. Loving and peacemaking are not merely sacrificing yourself for others. If you attain the power of your true self, you will be the first beneficiary.

Then your loving power, unlike the egoic energy you would use in order to possess other people's love for you in return, will not be caught in the phenomenon of the net of the egoic binary opposition. It is free to choose either pole of the opposites and expresses itself for others appropriately under the circumstances. In the midst of daily business, even though you are very busy, you would feel free, love for others, compassion for others, and peace. It means that your true self has no desire as your ego does—the desire that is a craving for recognition. In the sense that it is also activity (emptiness as movement), the true self is the pure desire without the wish to be recognized by others—not to be gratified with acknowledgment. After all, it has no cause and no result, no beginning and no end. It is *Emptiness as fullness*. That is the real you.

1.3. How literature and film pursue the ultimate reality

Q: How do you link meditation and literature? I have not found many who directly talk about meditation and literature, except a few spiritual teachers who sometimes find a good theme or underlying sense of stillness and peace in some poems. Is that your purpose as well?

No! I have *quite a different intention*. The most critical issues under discussion in this book continue with the spiritual and philosophical subjects in literature and film. However, my work of linking the artworks of literature, films, and meditation is quite different from that which others have previously done. As you said, people have usually employed poetry in order to promote the theme of stillness as the meditative state. In contrast, I take the path of deconstructing the theme, whether it is a novel, a poem, or a drama. This kind of postmodern or deconstructive work has been done in literary criticism, but while I was conducting academic research, writing, and teaching, as well as practicing Buddhist meditation and participating in Christian church services, I always kept the same purpose. I was also constantly trying to synthesize all these different areas for one goal—the ultimate reality of all of us and the world/universe.

I am convinced that we can encounter the true self as we read a literary text or watch a film. It would further help the readers of this book lead meditative daily lives with deep, genuine happiness. It is beyond question that if you have the habit of dwelling in the dimension of the true self, you will better manage your daily business. I am not simply saying that the meditative mental state will bring you worldly success in life. You first have to be detached from the hustle and bustle of life, and when you keep your composure, you can come to make it a habit to stay in the presence of deep self, and you will gain insight into life as you begin to think and behave with wisdom, rather than depend upon immediate success or failure.

Nonetheless, we have to employ such language of discernment and value judgment to make it clear that the true self, or the real I, is not the "false self," for which another name is the "ego." You can taste true spirituality when you are unconditionally open to what is not part of "me." Thought or intellectual knowing in itself cannot really manifest true spirituality. Your intellectual activity does not reach beyond its limit. That space over the inside-outside boundary is the realm of spirituality: it does not adhere to either side, but it embraces both. As our mind reaches beyond its capacity, it loses its grasp of clarity. In other words, in that realm of spirituality, intellectuality has no power. Rev. Seungsahn, a world-famous Korean Seon master who was considered as one of the "four living Buddhas" when he was alive (1927-2004), describes spirituality with the phrase, "don't-know mind." *Surrendering* the ego to its other is a unique way of being truly spiritual and free.

I will present how ethical deconstruction works for meditation, especially in the Buddhist style, in the following chapters. However, I would first like to demonstrate a rather thematic approach to the well-known Hollywood film *Forrest Gump* (1994). The film shows someone who stays with the special nature of honesty and warm-heartedness and overcomes his intellectual disability. He cannot even understand social rules and customs, and thus others make fun of him. Yet he does not struggle with himself and become disheartened too much. He could not run because his legs were weak, but one day he started running from the bullying guys. Later on, he becomes a very good football player, and when his mother dies and his girlfriend Jenny leaves him, he starts running. Then he runs for 3 years, 2 months, 14 days, and 16 hours across the entire United States.

I would like to say that he runs from the world of egos. The film offers us an opportunity to learn that a person of true wisdom belongs to spirituality that is uncontaminated by egoic feelings such as jealousy, greed, suffering, and pain, as well as shallow happiness and fun. In view of the ultimate reality, such egoic feelings go with insensitivity and unconsciousness. As in the Bible story of the first humans, gaining clear knowledge is simply decorating the outside of the fictitious shell of the ego, the false self. In fact, you can have an awakening experience without clearly knowing, or with some sublime bliss or joy. After this kind of spiritual experience, you will certainly be put in a better mental situation, although you will not find perfectly practical solutions to the troubles you experience. It is no exaggeration to say that spirituality is the true ground of intellectuality.

As many philosophers, including Nietzsche, have claimed, art has taken the role of religion in the modern age. Reading literary texts and appreciating other works of art can give the audience more spiritual power than religions that can fill believers' minds with the phenomenal notions and images of the supreme existence that governs the world with poetic justice. Throughout this whole book, and in the latter parts in particular, I will be guiding you on how to read literary masterpieces and watch great films in order to encounter and accept the universal true self, which is none other than the true God who both transcends time and space and works for you within time and space.

To take one more example, the ego can be described as the machine that controls humans, like the machine in *The Matrix* (1999). We *are* machines, as long as we suffer from the mentality of binary oppositions. Humanity will be set free when we are not attached to egoic decision-making due to which we blind ourselves to the dimension of true liberty. We are expected to let God in us be God, so to speak. The dimension of God's divinity, or the genuinely pure dimension of our life, lies beyond the nature of the ego, and we can let God be God only when we free our humanity from the ego—the separate self that feels isolated from others and thus suffers from various emotions. As it compares itself with outside objects, the separate, individual self comes to have pleasure and pain, excitement and depression, anger and attachment, pride, jealousy, fear, conflict, anxiety, superiority, and inferiority. Buddhism teaches us that those feelings produced by the ego construct have no deep and lasting value and that we should try to find the spiritual dimension of the one, or the ultimate reality. The spiritual dimension is unknown to the ego and thus transcends all such feelings that arise through the ego's structure of binary opposition.

In relation to literature and film, the sublime is the aesthetic motif of paramount importance. The sublime moment gives the reader the power to go beyond the theme that is limited to moral justice. By this, I mean postmodern ethical justice, not any obscuring topic that allows exotic thoughts and behaviors.

Literary texts, at least masterpieces, first clearly show us that the ego is fundamentally dualistic. Duality is the form of its existence. Precisely because its form is dualistic, it is an illusion that has no substance. The ego has no ability to realize the solid fact that there is stable ground between the polar opposites. The Transmiddle ground only looks unstable to the ego, which believes that its thinking, judging, and decision-making create a stable and normal ground. For example, the ego likes to decide on doing something—especially something that it thinks is rational. Now, as I explain in detail at the beginning of the next chapter, in the long period of human history, men have maintained male chauvinism, thinking that such decision-making of the male nature (decidability) is rational and looking down on the female nature (undecidability) as unstable. But contemporary postmodern ethicists, as well as ancient sages like Buddha, Laozi, and Zhuangzi, highly regard the female nature of undecidability.[4]

It is fundamentally very difficult for ordinary people to reach beyond egoic judgment. People have a strong egoic attachment to sticking to their own thoughts and feelings. The Buddhist term for ordinary humans and animals is "sentient beings" because they are attached to self-centered

---

[4] I have explored the nature of undecidability in great detail in my book, *Postmodern Ethics, and Literature: Encounters between East and West*, which is strictly academic. First, see Lee, *Postmodern Ethics*, 43, 60, 123. On undecidability with regard to reading a literary text, Mary Shelley's *Frankenstein*, see ibid., 217 and 221-222.

emotions and reasoning capacity. They are confused to the extent that they do not become aware when their mind is breaking the limits of their narrow ego. For example, they ignore their desire to know more about what seems to lie beyond their workaday experience—whether literary, artistic, or religious. Many usually disregard all but matters of money and pleasure. Yet, in fact, they have the genuine desire to know their true self and to live as such, although they do not know—at least not keenly. I would like to help them to turn their attention to their pure desire and become truly happy by reading literary texts and watching films.

1.4. The 2020 Oscar-winning films *Parasite* and *Joker*

Q: From what you said, I understand that literary works and films lead us through the aesthetic sublime to the ultimate reality. You also cited some examples. Now, would you show how Parasite *and* Joker, *two 2020 Academy Award-winning films, influence the viewer? The two movies use the same kind of material—class struggle, or the conflict between upper and lower classes in a capitalist society. I am very curious about how they work in light of your theory.*

You have a fantastic comprehension of our discussion. I am happy to elaborate. It is appropriate that we discuss *Parasite* (2019)[5] and *Joker*[6] (2019) before I explore more classical literary works and films in later chapters. You are right. *Parasite* and *Joker* are excellent movies that deal with class struggle, which has been the central social concern in all time periods, and yet is a more heated social issue in modern capitalist society that unavoidably brings violence. This issue of the rich and poor is not only the dual social structure; it is absolutely deeply rooted in the problem of the ego's inevitable structure of binary opposition.

The two films share this same issue. First, *Parasite* is a South Korean movie that won four awards at the Oscars in 2020—Best International Feature Film, Best Original Screenplay, Best Director, and even Best Picture. That is not all there is to talk about. It is amazing that this was the first time a non-English film won the Oscar for Best Picture!

This film deserves praise and admiration in other aspects such as editing, yet I think its forte is that all its elements are synthesized for the audience. Director Bong Joon-ho was able to do this job extremely successfully. First,

---

[5] Directed by Bong Joon-ho, produced by Kwak Sin-ae, written by Bong Joon-ho, screenplay by Bong Joon-ho, and starring Song Kang-ho and Han Jin-won.
[6] Directed, produced, and written by Todd Phillips, and starring Joaquin Phoenix, Robert De Niro, Zazie Beetz, and Frances Conroy.

there is the outward main issue or theme—the conflict between rich and poor that has seemingly been the most distinct issue of human society from ancient times to this day. It is also the most social issue in every country the world over—the United States or any other country is no exception.

Second, there are ample amounts of metaphors and symbols for the clearly set social hierarchy. The rich family lives in a high place, and the poor family in a semi-basement. The wealthy Park family members smell the semi-basement odor that Ki-taek (the father) and his family carry. The poor Kim family succeed in infiltrating the Park's world by taking jobs as different people—the housekeeper, the tutor, and the driver (Ki-taek)—and live like parasites. Then there is another even lower class of people, the former housekeeper and her husband, Geun-sae, living in a small cell-like bunker located in the lowest part of the mansion. The Kims and Geun-sae try to harm each other, and Ki-taek finally kills Mr. Park.

However, the most important element of this film as an artwork is the all-embracing sublime sensitivity that we come to experience in the last scenes. Before the outdoor party for Mr. Park's young son, violence breaks out in the small bunker as Geun-sae harms Ki-taek's son, who is in a slightly higher parasite position in this house himself. That is to say, violence ascends from the underground bunker to the worst positioned parasite. It then pervades the rest of the movie, revealing the middle zone between upper and lower classes where the dual social structure (binary opposition) is simply there without changing anything. Geun-sae kills Ki-taek's daughter, and Ki-taek kills Mr. Park, the rich man, yet the violence does not change the social hierarchy. The dimension of the sublime is simply reality without judgment. The dual structure produced by egos is just there without a revolutionary result of becoming different.

In fact, the whole movie is in that mood of changing but not changing. Director Bong is a master at exposing this space of equity and equanimity. In this sense, Park's family first appears as a host for parasites, yet they also live like parasites that suck the blood out of the bodies of the poor people that they look down upon. In fact, the upper and lower classes are mixed, and the difference is blurred. In this story, as well as metaphors and symbols, a new space assembles where all elements of the film mesh together. That tiny space, which actually pervades the entire film, allows us to have sublime sensitivity. Those sublime feelings we experience form the gate to the other side of the social situation of the class conflict produced by egos. Through this dimension of the middle zone where there is no hierarchy, we can experience the sublimity approaching our true self, which endlessly creates "egoistic" (as far as its basic frame is described) thoughts in the phenomenal world—like a *dancing light*. This sublime enjoyment is the delight of being one with the light of truth.

It is characteristic of this film that throughout its entirety, there is neither communication nor too much animosity between the upper and lower classes. The movie simply shows the space where they exist together. The sublime does not bring active enjoyment; it only lets us, the audience, realize the fundamental fact of being there.

Joker, which won two Oscars for Best Actor and Best Original Score, brings this problem of upper and lower classes to a more individual and psychological dimension. Violence plays a great role in this movie to capture the audience's attention. Arthur Fleck, the protagonist, is a failed stand-up comedian who is isolated, despised, and bullied by society. He finds out that his mental disturbance was caused by trauma. His mother, Penny, adopted Arthur as a baby, and one of her boyfriends and Penny herself violently abused him, which caused him to continuously laugh at inappropriate times. It seems possible in the movie that Thomas Wayne, a very rich candidate for mayor, is his biological father. Thomas never treats Arthur with compassion. We see that Arthur is only a victim of cruel people without compassion for others.

Arthur transforms into the Joker as he determines to, saying, "I used to think that my life was a tragedy, but now I realize, it's a comedy." He was striving to fight for his tragic life, but he gave way to violence. He lets go of his attachment to inferiority and accepts himself as such. At the same time, Arthur's killing of three men working for Thomas Wayne causes demonstrations against the upper class. Protesters wearing clown masks follow Arthur, their hero. As he is now a villain, violence prevails in society. The movie, via the phenomenon of violence, takes the audience on to the level of the *sublime sensitivity of freedom* that leads them beyond any expressions. As in *Parasite,* violence does not significantly change the social hierarchy in this film. The work aims to expose the dimension of liberty. As the movie ends, we come to experience the joyful *dance with the Joker,* entering into *the dancing light* of our true self that is beyond peace and violence. The light of truth *dances*—engendering all phenomena in the world.

Nevertheless, *Joker* brings a little too much violence in comparison to *Parasite.* Too much violence may cause an unstable effect on the social domain, but the movie is an artwork, not a tool to lay bare any social ideology. The aesthetic sublime opens our hearts to the dimension where everything is allowed. Yet, of course, the sublime is limited to being phenomenal as long as it is expressed. That is why there is a danger of crimes being committed by Joker imitators. What is *most important* is that our sublime sensibility goes *beyond* the upper-lower class conflict issue. The bliss of realizing the nuclear depth of life comes to us from *beyond* any reasoning or emotion. *We, the audience, experience real liberty from the egoic attachment only as we meditate on what the ultimate reality that the movie offers us is.* In later chapters, I will explain how we practice meditation with literary works and films.

Although it is the source of the ego, the true self seems only to know itself and not such objects as work and money. It does not respond to events in the way the ego does. However, it is always the source of the power of genuine wisdom to deal with both the problems of life and concrete situations. The egoic self, twisted and contaminated with a way of thinking, love as attached feeling, hate, jealousy, superiority, and inferiority, can dissolve, and the non-dual nature of the true self can prevail over the mind and body. The state of cowardice and indolence will evolve into a healthy state of having a clear purpose, insights on how to handle things, and diligence. This wholesome self is characteristic of "non-duality." Non-duality, or "not one, not two," is a better way of describing the ultimate reality than "oneness," in that one or oneness might implicate the sense of totalitarianism. Postmodern ethics and Buddhism, whose whole tradition has pursued the true self or no self, are effective in exploring these issues.

CHAPTER TWO

THE PROBLEM WITH THINKING:
WESTERN METAPHYSICS, LITERATURE,
AND FILM

Although throughout this book I illuminate and explain meditation and how to attain and continue to stay in the meditative state of mind by reading literature and watching films, I would first like to guide you through the basic framework and nature of thinking. In this chapter, I will discuss the problem of the ego that pretends to be the unique self, which has the great power of reasoning and finest judgment. This discussion will no doubt lead us to the depth of the true nature of our self. I will try my best to do my work in plain language, avoiding academic clichés, jargon, and such tones as much as possible.

Western philosophy has been struggling with itself to find, learn, and pursue the ultimate reality. Yet it has been commonly acknowledged that the main problem has been caused by the fact that it has almost always been *intellectually* done. The way to find the ultimate reality could not be done with intellectual ways of using reason and logic. In the first place, reason and logic are unable to carry the substantial essence. Rather, they are components of the mechanism of the ego defending itself from outside forces. Intellectualization is performed on the basis of the emotions of the ego itself, and thus it is the complexity of the unconsciously stressed mental activities, not of the pure and clear consciousness.

2.1. The problem with thinking and reasoning

Since the times of Plato and Aristotle, both of whom planted great faith in reason in Western thought, thinkers including such greats as Thomas Aquinas (1225-1274), René Descartes (1596-1650), Immanuel Kant (1724-1804), Georg Hegel (1770-1831), and Martin Heidegger (1889-1976), until the emergence of postmodernism, pursued universal "Reason," the best level of the mind to proceed to think according to "logos" (God's word that governs the cosmos), applying logic and other principles of rationality.

Western metaphysics has always identified Reason as the Idea, the highest spirit, the cosmic principle. Traditional Western philosophy and theology, before postmodernism, had been the study of generally accepted reasons and meanings. However, in fact, it is correct to say that although reason often gives thinkers "fruitful inspiration," "the attempt to push rational inquiry obstinately to its limits is bound often to fail, and then *the dream of reason* which motivates philosophical thinking seems merely a mirage."[7]

Truth as the ultimate reality cannot really be called something of "reason" or explained in a reasonable way. Reason is only the human capacity to consciously know and explain phenomenal cause and effect, and it is the grounds for a judgment according to them, but it is not the transcendental power to predict what will happen in the future and to control or influence a series of events or how others think and behave. That is, the nature of reason as an explanation of how something is caused to happen does not deserve to be described as something of the utmost importance or divinity. The true nature of reason and thinking is *impermanent* and *lacks true substance,* while the ego believes what it thinks is its substance. The true substance is not some nature of the tangible, solid, and stable presence. Reason is not the human faculty that explains all phenomena as Western thinkers thought in this line. There is no all-embracing supreme Reason as the ultimate causer.

In his *The Dream of Reason: A History of Western Philosophy* about the nature of Western thought, Anthony Gottlieb points out that at the dawn of Western philosophy, Plato believed that the faculty of reason is characteristic of the human soul and that, with the divine and universal nature, it exists "before birth and would continue after death."[8] Aristotle also declared that reason was the best faculty we have in pursuing the highest happiness and even immortality (despite his belief that reason would not outlive the cessation of life in the body).[9] After these two forebears, reason remained the *pivotal* matter in the tradition of Western philosophy—with its obvious flaw overlooked. In this age of postmodernism, it has been agreed far and wide that the lifeline of Western metaphysics is *reason*. Whenever we describe the innate nature of the tradition of Western metaphysics and theology, whether it be its virtue or weakness, the first terms employed would be "reason," "rationality," "logic," and "logos." Those terms characterize the same nature—the high-level capacity for thinking on a clearly explainable ground or with an understandable motive.

---

[7] Anthony Gottlieb, *The Dream of Reason: A History of Western Philosophy* (New York: W. W. Norton & Company, 2016), xii, emphasis added.
[8] Ibid., 237.
[9] Ibid.

2.2. An example of the problem with discernment
in the Book of Genesis

Nevertheless, I would like to claim that *"reason" itself is not what Western metaphysics really strived for.* It is my conviction that human thought, by its very nature, even unknowingly, seeks to attain, or be one with, the transcendental power of genuine liberty from events, others, and also from their ego. Especially from the perspective of postmodern ethics, I propose that Western thinkers have actually investigated the exteriority of human subjectivity, whereas their methods were innately natured to be dualistically built on the basis of reason, the ability to judge the value of phenomena that seem to take place outside. In this state, the I sees itself as an object itself only as it confronts an object outside. It does not see the inside. Nevertheless, its goal is the exterior.

The thoughts of Parmenides (515 BC-?) and Socrates (470?-399 BC) are now widely acknowledged to be very close to those of Eastern sages. Parmenides thought that the true reality was formless and lay beyond the illusory form of the world.[10] Socrates, who inherited this style of thought, was known to contemporary scholars as an enlightened human like Shakyamuni (or Siddhārtha Gautama) Buddha and the Ch'an/Seon/Zen masters.[11] But Socrates left no writing, and consequently, Plato, his student, was not able to fully understand and follow his spiritual accomplishment. Plato's emphasis on reason has since been handed down to Western philosophers.

Since this time, the capacity of reasoning is what Western metaphysics has valued so dearly throughout its entire tradition. "Reason" is not just the human ability to calculate the advantages and disadvantages of doing something. Even imperceptible transcendence or infinity has been conceived of as the realm of highest reason. We find such places of reason, thoughts, and ideas from Plato to Descartes, Kant, and Hegel. The thinkers took reason in general as the fundamental human faculty of handling all knowledge and phenomena.

However, again we find, as Levinas did, that such great Western philosophers as Plato and Descartes did not end up emphasizing reason. It is clear to me that they did pursue transcendence beyond phenomena and the status of genuine self-realization. Descartes was an essentially great supporter of *infinity*. In this era of postmodernism, and more specifically postmodern ethics, the most prominent contemporary Western thinkers such

---

[10] William Bodri, *Socrates and the Enlightenment Path* (Boston: Red Wheel/Weiser, 2001), 5.
[11] Ibid., 5.

as Emmanuel Levinas, Jacques Derrida, Jean-François Lyotard (who declared this is a postmodern age), Jean-Luc Nancy, Giorgio Agamben, Antonio Negri, and others are all serious about humanity itself, rather than simple illusory phenomena and facts.

It seems to me that for American and Western readers, the best way to begin is by turning to the beginning of the Judaic and Christian Bible that refers to God's creation. On the one hand, the Christian Bible as a whole tells us about God as the highest being—an object outside. Yet it does not end there. On the other hand, it presents God to us as the ultimate spiritual state of ourselves. The story of the first humans in the Old Testament seems to be the best place to discuss this understanding that is set in the dualism that divides our mind conceptually into two opposites—the subject and the object.

It is the state of Adam and Eve in Paradise—the primal human nature. As described in the Book of Genesis, the first humans were expelled from Paradise because they ate the fruit of the tree of the knowledge between good and evil and gained the ability to judge between what they like and dislike and choose either one. The dualistic mind is born as the original sin against God. God and the human mind were one in Paradise. However, here is an important point that I should like to bring up. First, let us take a look at the crucial part of Genesis:

> God blessed them; and God said to them, "Be fruitful and multiply, and fill the earth, and subdue it; and rule over the fish of the sea and over the birds of the sky and over every living thing that moves on the earth." (Gen. 1:28)

Let us pause and give a thought to this. How can humans multiply without knowledge of good and evil, of all desire, including sexual desire? It is impossible for us even to start thinking about anything. Now, I am not saying that Adam and Eve already had enough faculty to judge between good and evil in Paradise. I would claim with absolute certainty that they had the *minimal* reasoning faculty in their original state already. Eating the fruit of the tree of knowledge of good and evil is the surplus, the excess, of that capacity. The excess is the outflowing force of the ego. In Paradise, Adam and Eve had the pure, nuclear power of judging and measuring the values of objects outside. They had the appropriate amount of reasoning capacity. The result of their desire to have more wisdom than that reduced the pure state of their mind and brought them a loss of security, fear, anxiety, hate, jealousy, loneliness, and only superficial feelings of happiness.

Of course, Adam and Eve's state of mind reflects the primary mind, which is prior to any doing or thinking. This purity beyond, behind, beneath, or prior to the concepts of pure and impure is the ultimate reality. The ultimate reality is the reality of God's mind—omniscient and omnipresent in the whole universe. The pre-original state of the human mind is, if not God's mind itself, a copy of it. That is why it is said humankind was created in God's image (Gen. 1:27).

This story of the beginning of human history reflects that as one grows up after birth, the intensity of the surplus of the correct amount of reasoning capacity grows and is cultivated through human relations and education in the given culture. The expulsion from Paradise means that one is separated from the purity that lies beyond the intensity of reasoning. The pure faculty of reasoning in itself is not lost but is still in all of us. Rather, it is just contaminated by the various sorts of surplus. The purest mind is the mind that stands alone. It is the ultimate reality we are expected to reside within. Yet the surplus of reasoning capacity leads us to think that we lost the purity and became separated from God's image, that is, from the perfectness of the transcendental mind. But in fact, we still have that capacity in the deepest part of our mind. More than that, it is always using its capacity for creation in daily life. God consciousness is truly all that our life takes! You as an individual and the whole universe are one, and that is it!

The crucial point for ourselves is not whether we religiously have to express that humans were punished by being expelled from Paradise. We rather always have to remember that we have Paradise in our mind. To realize the truth that Paradise is in our mind first means that the ultimate reality is down here in the presence of our life, not up there as some ideal existence. It is the power of the creation of the concrete presence of everybody, everything, and every phenomenon. We are lost in the midst of vain and unreliable desires only when we deny the fact that we are in Paradise. In the ultimate reality, we are not lost, but our ego always enjoys pleasures and pain. We suffer the results of our own desires that appear in the form of happiness and pain, but the absolute good lies beyond ideas of good and evil (or bad), right and wrong, high and low. These concepts are formed with egoic perspectives in different societies and cultures and are valid in the realm of phenomena. But as long as we are attached to phenomena, we go back and forth between pleasure/happiness and pain/suffering. Sensuous pleasure and superficial happiness are actually no different from pain and suffering.

Therefore, this fundamental human problem of transcending or overcoming desire cannot be solved by any ideas, concepts, or explanations because ideas, concepts, and explanations only take the side of the presence of an existence. Paradise inside us cannot be reached with thought, language, or any other kind of expression. God, Paradise, or the ultimate reality is absolutely above all expressions and experiences, whether the object of the expression is the presence or absence of any state. As in the Bible, God's face is not sensibly seen. One of the best examples is what God says to Moses when he asks God to show His face: "You cannot see My face, for no man can see Me and live!" (Ex. 33:20).

The ultimate reality, or pure awareness, is not of the sort that is reachable by way of perceiving and discerning what you see, touch, feel, or think. When one's ego justifies one's experience with reason, what it is really doing is fabricating what it experienced. In other words, all animate beings and inanimate things are manifestations of God. God consciousness, which is most general, is formless and empty, and that is why genuine transcendence is the actual power of shaping every being, every thing, and every phenomenon. Again, it is also beyond the state that can be called the "absence" of anyone, anything, or any phenomenon. We can reach genuine transcendence only by dropping any possibility of any sort of expression. To put it otherwise, it is the most fundamental one that produces forms and destroys forms, the most profound ground where every being, every thing, and every phenomenon arises and disappears. We can approach it only as we let go of the ego's desire, even the desire to attain the state of pure awareness with the discerning mind.

Of course, reason and emotion work together in making a decision. Emotion strengthens the reasoned decision just as cement attaches different objects together. Attachment is the work of the ego: it is the emotional tendency to seam the natural phenomena of the split in the ego. As the dreamer believes the dream is real, so does the ego simply accept life without any doubt. The ego has the mere function of perceiving objects (phenomena included) only as it interprets them for its own sake. It misunderstands its own childish interpretation as the result of the normal activity of the mind. Unlike a mirror which reflects any form it happens to meet, the ego covers, adorns, or distorts objects with its own taste. It twists and fabricates the vision as it arrives from pure awareness.

Like the state of a clear mirror, the ultimately natural awareness is the most genuine nature of all beings that live, all inanimate things, and all phenomena that take place in the world. But for the ego, the intensity of its attachment has to be reduced and eventually eliminated. What is needed is the *immediate judgment* that instantly divides the polar opposites—right and wrong, good and bad—in a *given situation*. The judgment happens only as a *natural result* of the *condition*. At the end of the day, the function of the judgment in a *given situation* is the only ability that the ego has to have. Eliminating the ego intensity means awakening from the dreamlike contextual nature of life. Once awakened, you would still have to keep trying to completely exterminate the habit of going back to have the ego intensity again.

The real I or the true self in itself is the purest and perfect awareness without the whirlpool of the ego intensity. In order to protect the audience from the danger of misunderstanding the real self, I would like to lay emphasis on the fact that without the features of the ego intensity such as anger, pleasure, happiness, sadness, jealousy, one will *live life fully and have the wisest judgment in each given condition.* It is never the kind of emotionally frozen state of mind that is not able to feel happiness, that would not enjoy living, or that would end in just living a moralistic life. It is the freest state of mind that feels the sublime feelings and is minded to help others.

But I would also like to stress that in Buddhism, *"no self"* means the *"real self" without the ego intensity.* The judging point would certainly be the best answer that naturally comes up for the present condition, which is also for the whole universe, without being trapped in the ego-made prison. To show you that no self is the real self, I would just like to introduce a phrase in the *Heart Sutra*; we will start to explore Buddhist philosophy in detail later on. The following line describes the state of Emptiness as fullness in a very concise way: "Form is emptiness, emptiness is form." Emptiness is expressed in all the different forms. True Emptiness, as I capitalize it, is perfectly void of any thought (concepts, ideas, images). From the Buddhist perspective, the ultimate reality is Emptiness, perfectly void of phenomena. It can never be set as an object of our cognition.

At this point, let me make clear that *I have no intention of promoting the doctrines of Buddhism as a religion.* In fact, "meditation" by its nature includes Christian contemplative/centering prayer, which has long been maintained, especially in the tradition of the Eastern Catholic Church. From an objective perspective, Emptiness (Sunyata), the goal of Buddhist meditation, can be seen as another name for the Kingdom of Heaven, Paradise, or God. Yet any kind of issue that can cause a religious argument is *not* one of the issues dealt with here in this book. In this way, the primary idea of "dualism" is the one that produces concepts. In the first place, dualism divides one reality into two—presence and absence. Beyond any doubt, this is not only a "Western" style of thinking: When it comes to this kind of human habit with "reason" and the "practicality" of making value judgments, it is most often called "Western." In academia, it is commonsensical that, on a larger style, this "reason"-centered thinking mode is characterized as a "Western" style, although reason has always played a great role throughout the whole of human history. However, in fact, all ordinary people almost always seem to be stuck to this way of thinking. They have no doubt that what is usually called the "reality" of their daily life just consists of what they see, hear, touch, and believe. That is why they are lost in spiritually meaningless or insignificant affairs and blind to broader views of the self, world, and universe. Such unconscious people are usually very interested in matters of money, fame, and so on, but not on issues of spirituality. (Yet they could be interested in cyborg matters.)

It is clear to me that after humans experienced the devastating result of the two world wars, prominent contemporary thinkers of postmodernism wars declared that Western metaphysics has only been described as the metaphysics of the "presence" of phenomena. In the field of Western academic philosophy, presence means only the state of phenomenal existence or an idea that can be known by the part of the human mind that cognizes, reasons, and proves it by language or other means.

It does not have the comprehensive meanings of "being" and "presence" that contemporary secular spiritual leaders refer to. I hope that readers will not misunderstand the meanings of those words as meant in two different areas. Although the two areas share the same ultimate purpose of knowing the highest reality, philosophy is an academic field and spiritual teaching signifies experience. Spiritual teachers, many of whom come from Buddhism, employ "being" and "presence" as words that indicate how an existence in itself is inside, as opposed to movement, which takes place outside. But traditional Western philosophers, and also their critics (when they reveal the weaknesses and demerits of the Western metaphysical tradition), employ the same words for the phenomenal state of an existence (in a sense, as God is usually understood in a representative way in Christianity and other religions). The critics of the metaphysics of presence mean the system of only the appearance of the present existence without a sense of spiritual quality as Emptiness that embraces both presence and absence and keeps a distance from both presence and absence. Thus, being and presence are used in *traditional Western philosophy* to justify the value of *reasoning* in the dualistic mode. In contrast, the spiritual leaders of today point to the whole of an existence or the whole of the universe, and they signify spirituality that indicates the human experience of the whole universe as one that touches us all.

It is truly unfortunate that the meanings of being and presence, as understood in the Western metaphysical tradition, do not transcend the limit of presence. In other words, Western metaphysics, however great its thinkers, has "strangely" been restricted to the prison of human thinking, mainly due to the responsibility that humans academically and scientifically prove their arguing points just on the grounds of reason. No doubt, reasoning is a dualistic thinking mode that separates the grounds of one common being into two, the subject and the object, and the subject judges the object from its perspective that has been constructed in personal history. One cannot deny that this is the Eurocentric idea of Georg Hegel. Yet in fact, even though the dualistic mode of thinking is just a common mode of human thinking, it is acknowledged that it is characterized by an especially Western style of thinking.

Contemporary thinkers of postmodernism or postmodern ethics agree that Western philosophy, in its tradition, has been characteristically dualistic and separated presence, being, and existence, and ignored the other side as nihilistic absence or non-existence. (Postmodernism, particularly postmodern ethics, ought not to be miscomprehended and simply dismissed as the "anything goes" type of thinking.) To put it in another way, Western thought as a whole has been too practical and scientific, benefitting from the raw reality of what can be seen, thought, and pursued. In our scientifically and technologically highly developed world, we appreciate the merits of this style of thinking.

You may say that Western thought as a whole has involved the work of an "intellectual" understanding of phenomena. "Intellectuality" is the state or quality of the mental or intellectual ability of thinking as the brain's function, while through "spirituality" we desire to reveal what lies beyond thinking and language and try to be one with it. "Spirituality" leads us to the meaning of life and the ultimate reality as the universal human experience. For example, in terms of mentality, you can say there are so many truths of different forms of events, instead of one truth that dominates the world. But spiritually, there is no truth at all, in that life is like a dream in which everything has no stable meaning, or there is the one, non-phenomenal truth, and thus "form is emptiness and emptiness is form."

But again, it is surely not restricted to being a problem of the tradition of the Western mode of thought. We usually believe that reason has to take the highest position in whatever we do—whether it be in an individual case or an event of a group, society, or nation. Examples can be easily taken from our mundane daily conversations: "What are the reasons you are doing that?"; "Do you have an unknown reason for that special kind of thing?"; "Be careful not to lose the power of reason." In war, soldiers easily lose their rational minds and become "like beasts." For many who are simply used to conventional and routine ways of thinking and behaving, it is extremely difficult to allow themselves to step forward from the habit of reasoning.

The meaning of reason shown by the extremely simple examples given above has the advantage of pursuing a clear purpose of our thinking and acting. We really need logical thinking in such areas as law and scientific research and experimentation. Indeed, no one can deny the development of those fields in the West. However, Western thought in general has been limited to ontology, the study of existence, being as opposed to nihilistic nothing. In Buddhism and Taoism, what transcends reason, emotion, and language was already thoroughly studied in ancient times. Now is the time Easterners and Westerners should cooperate not only to make the world a place to live with better technology but to live with better situations and methods for spiritual awakening. Literature and films are the two greatest and easiest ways of reaching the ultimate reality.

If humans only end up developing technologically and producing programs and artificial intelligence, our subjective, egoic mind will not do a better job than just perceiving what takes place around us. For those people in that state of mind, it would be too big a leap to acknowledge and positively accept the infinity of the true self that lies over the finitude of reason, rationality, and emotions that go with them. Their minds are closed to what transcends reason, emotion, and what is accepted and passes for common sense. The genuine transcendence that lies beyond phenomenality is the infinite, and it pervades all finite beings. It is a total misunderstanding to think "genuine transcendence" is not simply "mystical."

As is well known, the Western concept of "philosophy" stems from the Greek word "*philosophia*," which is a compound word of "*philos*" (love) and "*sophia*" (wisdom). Yet the tradition of Western philosophy as the love of wisdom shows that thinkers have understood wisdom as the capability to *conceptually* understand and judge what is phenomenally true, right, or moral in given concrete situations using knowledge, experience, and common sense. In this sense, traditional Western philosophy could be called the study of wise living, and as a result, it has ignored the emptiness of phenomena.

There have been prominent postmodern ethicists such as Lyotard, Levinas, Nancy, Deleuze, Badiou, and Agamben in the latter part of the 20th century, and now in the early part of the 21st century, their influence on academia is still immense. Whoever may be interested in postmodernism or postmodern ethics will easily find that such words as "reason," "intellectuality," and "discernment" for decision-making are not as important as they were before. The new task of thinking is represented by such ideas as "undecidability," "indeterminacy," "infinity," "infinite movement," "the other" (as what is other than the self), and "the wholly other." The point is laid in the middle between two polar opposites that build judgment by the power of the ego construct.

In fact, the concepts of "reason," "intellectuality," and "impermanence" delineate the boundary of an existence or phenomenon whose nature is finite, and "infinity" or "spirituality" indicates the dimension beyond the reach of finitude. In the sense that finitude or infinity is not the nature of absence but the character of some present realm that we can understand and accept, albeit as an abstract idea, we can say that finitude *describes* a small unity or step of infinity. A limitless number of small unities make the succession of its consequences look like it is approaching infinity. From this commonly acceptable perspective, and with reference to the infinite, true self is in the finite ego, and the ego somehow manifests the infinite self.

This is not only the case for managing individual daily life. People strongly tend to think this way not only in their own lives but in national and international affairs, and we often witness horrible wars arising out of this collective egoism. As we look back on human history and what is happening in the world now, we clearly see decisions made with the power of the ego construct have caused problems without limits. Usually, we humans tend to believe that our reasoning mind works almost perfectly, if not wholly perfectly, as the ground for our judgments and decisions, and we tend to ignore other possibilities that we would not immediately go for.

It seems that infinity and finitude are not really separable but supplement each other, and in the final view, they are one. Infinity takes the form of the present moment, and the ego's function of thinking is not merely transient and impermanent. In the same manner, "reason" has constructed the Western style of expressing the essence of thinking that goes beyond its conventional sense for infinity. As Western thinkers have steadfastly insisted, the ultimate Reason would have to be the supreme providence or dispensation of the all-embracing One. The ultimate Reason is the One, which means the connections of all reasons that make possible the continuation of animate beings, inanimate things, and even time and space.

2.3. Is infinity itself the other side of binary opposition and reason?

So, are we simply finite beings whose lives have no ultimate spiritual value? Absolutely not! In fact, our finite thinking and acting are expressions of the infinity of the ultimate reality. On the one hand, we first have to acknowledge that infinity in itself never belongs to the dimension of time and space. Infinity lies entirely beyond the dimension of time and space. On the other, infinity is not separable from infinite or endless movement. Relating endless movement as a scholar in the contemporary world of philosophy and literary criticism, I understand this problem of reason and rationality in terms of the conflicts arising from the form called "binary opposition." Rationality, on the basis of reason, which easily seems to be in a higher position than emotion regarding factuality, works to tie the polar opposites that construct a thought. I have elaborated on binary opposition in great detail through the whole of my previous work, *Postmodern Ethics, Emptiness, and Literature: Encounters between East and West*, with reference to both Eastern and Western philosophies. Bringing up the thoughts of Descartes, Nietzsche, Hegel, and Heidegger and of ethical thinkers of postmodernism such as Derrida, Lyotard, Nancy, and especially Levinas as the greatest postmodern ethicist, I first examined the weakness of Western philosophy as ontological philosophy, which would collapse without the work of conceptualization, ontological judgment, and linguistic meaning. The focus of my discussion is laid on how those postmodern ethicists tried to overcome the problem of *binary opposition*, and presents my view of how thought in Mahayana Buddhism, especially Ch'an/Seon/Zen, could advance Western ethics and literary criticism.

In this way, in the present work, I try to elaborate on binary opposition, not simply for its meaning but with the purpose of dissolving it in the spiritual experience of glimpsing and encountering "infinity" through reading literature, watching films, and appreciating other arts. For the average person, who does not think about genuine spiritual liberty, contemplating spirituality or the spiritual dimension is so difficult because it is out of reach of the capacity of human reason, which is possible only in terms of the mental mirroring systems called cognition, perception, or knowing. The mental process of becoming aware of an object is possible precisely because it is structured as a "binary opposition." Only through binary opposition can one's mind have knowledge of the object, whether it is mental or physical. However, the result of the mental process that goes through binary opposition has a firm limitation; it is unable to go beyond binary opposition.

Yet we need to go one step deeper into our own consciousness, into humanity itself. Why is there ever binary opposition? First of all, binary opposition means the split in oneness, and it indicates the beginning of movement. If one's mind has only one tendency, it would not understand and accept other inclinations and other states of mind. For example, if you like only pleasant feelings, you would not have the power to accept unhappiness. Then you would not enjoy life as a whole. The deepest part of our mind—that is, the purest consciousness beyond the concepts of purity and impurity—does not exclude the nature of binary opposition. The minimal form of binary opposition is actually the source of the great power to produce and change/improve situations in our lives. If we do not get attached to either of the opposites, the structure of binary opposition makes possible God's infinite movement of creation through us! It empowers us to generate new ideas and to condition new situations. The least phenomenality of binary opposition gives birth to every existence! That is to say, the truly transcendent God always continues to create new forms in the flow of finite time and space by touching on the phenomenality. However, the human ego expands what is necessary and enjoys dreaming. God's infinity is above and beyond the finitude of time and space.

Thus, infinity is not separable from finitude. It seems that infinity does not allow itself to be clearly revealed by anyone within the domain of time and space where everything is unstable and understood with transitory concepts. Yet the ultimate reality infinitely creates all movements and phenomena through binary opposition, which is the essence of movement. The infinite movement is the endless repetition of changes between right and wrong, good and evil, high and low. This means that the ultimate reality is phenomenally neither one nor two (subject-object): it is the One that embraces the whole, but it is not phenomenally one. It is already a curious, mysterious, abstruse movement. At the end of the day, being is already doing. That is how we can say that God is the most fundamental love that embraces both good and evil.

The infinity of the ultimate reality takes its form in the finitude of relative phenomena. The absolute love gives birth to existences and phenomena, whose nature is conceived of as good or evil. There is no substance or lasting identities of humans and other beings and things in the domain of existence and phenomena. The relative good cannot be identified as such without the concept of the other side, which is evil, and no one can characterize anything evil without the idea of good. Good and evil are the relatively identified natures. If we cling to reason and emotions that comprise our decision, we cannot see the absolute good, the whole.

Of course, we must not follow the examples of evil people or phenomena; we must pursue what we come to think is good for ourselves and others. But after all, as the design of the Tao shows, good and evil are one. The two are in one circle, *dual in non-duality*. The deepest part of each half is within the realm of the other, and it means that the two were originally one. They are one not only in terms of origin; they are always one in the transphenomenal dimension of the ultimate truth.

The life of every being, thing, and phenomenon is transient, illusory, and thus has no substance of being itself, and all judgments are, after all, the results of reasonable consideration—judging between good and evil, and it is profoundly for the self. The non-dual ultimate reality lies beyond the phenomenon of every being and every thing, and reasoning is an act that is done only in the realm of phenomena. Reasoning, evaluating, and comparing are acts of justifying one's thought or behavior, the way in which one acts or conducts oneself in the domain of binary opposition. Reasoning and creating values include every system of ideology, every system of every nation, and every system of religious dogmas.

The ultimate reality is the whole of the universe as all of space and time and is presented in the innermost part of our mind and being as the perfect love without egoic nature. In this light, we are all one in the transphenomenal love, which lies beyond the concepts of the polar opposites—love and hate, good and evil, purity and impurity. The form of opposition reflects that the ultimate reality is not some motionless state of truth but a lively movement of creative power. The Christian doctrine of the Trinity—the Father, the Son (Jesus Christ), and the Holy Spirit—indicates the ceaseless spiritual movement of creation in the dimension of phenomena. God is the movement that creates the most fundamental relations with differences produced by fundamental binary positions, not the conflict causing the egoic opposition structure. From the Taoist perspective, the most profound movement is like the power that moves Yin and Yang. Yin and Yang are opposites in one.

It is important that the ultimate reality does not have any stability. God is already transphenomenal or "quasi"-moving. The *Heart Sūtra* (Sanskrit *Prajñāpāramitāhṛdaya* or Chinese ☒ ☒ Xīnjīng), one of the primary and most popular texts in Mahayana Buddhism (in Northern Asian countries), says, "Emptiness is form, form is emptiness." This is because everything, even Dharma, the ultimate Truth of the cosmos, is a movement, and nothing is in a stable, fixed state. The Buddha has said, "I have taught for 50 years, but really taught nothing," and "Do things as if you do not do anything."

2.4. The worthless part of thinking is the ego intensity

It is correct to say that although reason often gives thinkers "fruitful inspiration," "the attempt to push rational inquiry obstinately to its limits is bound often to fail, and then the dream of reason which motivates philosophical thinking seems merely a mirage."[12] Vladimir Solovyov, a Russian, is well-known to have harshly criticized Western ideals of reason, especially "individual reason's war against nature," or more accurately, "the subordination of nature to reason in Western philosophy from Descartes to Hegel."[13] Solovyov says in his famous *The Crisis of Western Philosophy* that Descartes, "the first representative of modern philosophy," paved the idea of *cogito ergo sum,* positioning the authority of thinking as reason

---

[12] Gottlieb, *The Dream of Reason*, 237, xii.
[13] For the quotes from Solovyov in this paragraph, see Vladimir Solovyov, *The Crisis of Western Philosophy (Against the Positivists)*, trans. and ed. Boris Jakim (Hudson: Lindisfarne Press, 1996), 17-19.

above all: "for Descartes the external world can be recognized as having genuine reality only when such reality is demanded by reason." But then, "the truth of reason here does not depend on any external confirmation; rather, reason itself contains with itself the whole basis of its truth—*cogito ergo sum* ('I think, therefore I am')." Descartes' idea of reason excluded nature and reduced "the whole content of the external world to formal mathematical definitions" as he manipulated the relations between reason, thinking, body, and spirit.

Nevertheless, I would like to underline here that it is a misconception that thinking is wholly the product of the ego. In fact, the faculty of discernment in itself is the precious ability that we absolutely need. The point is that we do not need the surplus intensity of the ego. The formless infinity comes to take its form as an ego, one of the countless worlds, and so the ego is a varied form of pure consciousness or awareness, which is the ultimate reality. Yet the ego is an individual desiring machine and defense mechanism that only serves itself for its own good. The ego is a false self that denies finding satisfaction in the true reality. Another word to describe it is "fiction." There is no ego without thinking, and thus the ego is the unnecessary product of thinking. There is no thinking that has not arisen in the ground of the ego. The problem though is the excessive intensity of the swirling ego. The ego, which exists for itself, and the process of thinking cannot be separated, but the swirling is only an unneeded delusion. We just need the ability of the thinking mind without the whirlpool of delusion.

What I propose is that we must separate the point of the beginning of thinking, which is necessary, and the excessive amount of the ego, which is the tendency of being "attached" to its object. *It is not simply that the ego and thinking are one and whatever one thinks is egoic.* In addition, no doubt, there is the advantage of thinking in the Western style—in a word, being scientific, although being scientific in itself is not a means for a perfect life. I will get to this issue soon, but at this present moment, let us focus on the tight connection between the ego and thinking. Thinking is the process of the mind's oscillating movement between the two polar opposites. The ego as one's psychic activity would understand and accept only what it likes and hates or does not accept or embrace whatever it does not like. This endless process of choosing between what it favors and what it hates or dislikes is the ego's work of "thinking." We constantly think. As one wakes up in the morning, they start thinking about what will happen that day on the basis of their emotional responses to those they will meet and their memories of that person—all of these arise in their mind. They then go on to be full of themselves or lose the courage to manage their life using their own will to live happily in the way they want. They even take their thinking into their dream. It is not, as Descartes asserted, that only thinking has a certainty for living. "I think, therefore I am" is the law in a dream. To reach the ultimate reality, minimum thinking is enough; more than that would cause superficial happiness as excitement and pain.

As will be shown in great detail in the following chapters, Buddhism (and Taoism) has always been pursuing what lies beyond thinking. If we were to convert *cogito ergo sum* to a Buddhist form, it would be "I don't think, therefore I am." The real self is the transcendent source of the sensation and intellectualization that takes place in time and space. Thinking is impossible without the ego, the "self" that is constructed in the time of an infant, no matter how much it should be valued. Trusting the certainty of thinking, the ego's work as a process of producing ideas is not as reliable as Descartes believed. If there is no object that we must understand and accept, thinking is not only necessary but dangerous to making us more unconscious. The overtly bad result would be being narrow-minded and prejudiced.

In fact, even before the dawn of postmodernism, in the heart of philosophical discourses done in the 19th and 20th centuries, Western philosophers found faults with the Western way of philosophizing and went against it. Some supreme examples of Western metaphysics' self-criticism are the works of such thinkers as Friedrich Nietzsche and Martin Heidegger, who are at the heart of Western philosophy. Nietzsche took a very harsh attitude toward traditional moral values in Western philosophy, more specifically in Christian doctrines, and anticipated the desolation and end of traditional philosophy and theology. Nietzsche proclaimed such ideas as "the death of God" and "the eternal recurrence" in *The Gay Science* (1882), and also the very well known "will to power" in *The Will to Power* (1901). He thought that Christianity only offers the tenacity to stick to servile morality and cowardice instead of the courage to live fully in ethical terms.

Regarding Buddhism, Nietzsche first eagerly welcomed it, but later on misunderstood the Buddhist issue of "Emptiness" as that of nihilistic nothingness and dismissed Buddhism as a whole as a valueless, negative nihilism in *The Will to Power*. The primary point of his philosophy was "positive nihilism." Nonetheless, what he thought of as positive nihilism was close to the thought of Nagarjuna (c.150-c.250 AD), who restored and strengthened the true meaning of Emptiness following Shakyamuni Buddha and set up the doctrine of Emptiness. It is to live a fully free life without being attached to represented thoughts, which are conceptualized with reason and logic. At any rate, Nietzsche acknowledged the dimension of non-duality which lies beyond the domain of value judgment—good and evil, right and wrong.[14]

---

[14] See Lee, *Postmodern Ethics*, 5-6.

Around the time of the Second World War, Heidegger criticized the tradition of representational thinking based on reason and logic as having run its course, but then he walked the same path as Nietzsche. Heidegger's thought was ontology, a study of existence which could not go outside of the tradition of representational thinking, for which reasoning took the most vital role. Heidegger is well-known for his strong and lasting interest in Buddhism and Taoism. His thought was that Western philosophy had run its course because its representational mode had not revealed the difference between *Being* and *beings*. But this thought still shows the supreme identity in the different name of "Being." Heidegger simply replaced the world-dominating God with Being. Yet "Being" or "being" only indicates *presence*. In other words, what Heidegger meant by ontological difference is not fundamental.[15]

Despite all his appreciation of Eastern thought and interest in it, he only went back to, and even strengthened, traditional Western philosophy as a study of the appearance of the present existence. His famous question "Why are there beings at all instead of nothing?" shows where he stopped—at the depth of dualism.[16] Heidegger's question is more fundamental than traditionally handled issues, but it did not really overcome the problem of limitation. Western philosophers have focused their inquiries on the state of being alive, simply believing that the other side of being is nothingness, merely as the absence of being, and as a result, so did Heidegger.

At the present time of human history, we *truly* have to go back to the source of humanity and advance spirituality. Is it so important whether we are Westerners or Easterners? Being one species, why discriminate against each other? Do different races really like to look down on one another? If they do, you must realize the solid fact that the struggle is, first and foremost, right there in their own minds, which means that they hate themselves. As they hate the other, the bomb of hatred explodes in their own minds. Western philosophers, Heidegger included, have been *intellectually* and *not spiritually* serious about the Truth that they wanted to know. Such a way of comprehension reflects their fear of the exteriority of the zone of presence (in the philosophical meaning), which is the dimension of existence. Western metaphysics, in this way, has always been a study of existence, not taking a serious view of the real totality of presence and absence. Thus, Western philosophy has been a study of presence as opposed to absence. From the standpoint of such a mode of thought, it is no wonder

---

[15] Jacques Derrida, *Margins of Philosophy*, trans. Alan Bass (Chicago: University of Chicago Press, 1982), 22.
[16] Martin Heidegger, *Introduction to Metaphysics*, trans. Gregory Fried and Richard Polt (New Haven: Yale University, 2000), 1.

that the opposite of existence as non-being is considered as nihilistic nothingness with no value for life. The study of existence has always forgotten the substantial human need to explore spirituality, which is the most fundamental, incorporeal, and immaterial ground of life.

Contrastively, the attraction of Buddhism as a whole, and the Mahayana tradition in particular, lies in the fact that it presents us with what lies beyond the limited vision. Buddhism teaches us:

> Emptiness is a state that belongs neither to presence nor absence, that is, neither being nor non-being, neither something nor nothing. Emptiness can never be identified as something conceptually determinable as a state or condition. Emptiness or Tao, coming out of the middle path, makes possible, but also excludes, any conception."[17]

The genuinely fundamental (non-representable) dimension which lies beyond existence and non-existence cannot be an object of rational understanding: An open heart can accept spirituality without discerning.

However, in the late 20th and 21st centuries, there have been postmodern thinkers (philosophers and literary critics) whose thoughts have signified spirituality. They have studied and declared that the ego is the primary power that should be weakened and eventually abandoned. Lots of them are professors and artists in both the classical mode and the popular style and have presented the ways of deconstructing or destroying the structure of the ego construct and eliminating the ego intensity for the public. Moreover, there have been many secular spiritual leaders who have taught people to live in a state of spiritual liberation, or a deeply contented, joyful, and creative life with genuine wisdom. Many spiritual teachers of that kind are religious leaders. Their common idea is that we should lessen, if not remove, the power of the ego. Spirituality increases as the ego power lessens.

I will not explore what and how academic thinkers have been discussed regarding the self and the ego by going through the history of Eastern and Western ideas on the human mind here, for I have done that work in my previous book. For the understanding and miscomprehension of Buddhism by Western thinkers such as Hegel and Nietzsche, the discussion in Chapter One will help.

The main problems of Western metaphysics arise from its primary issue of the basic frame of human cognition called *binary opposition*, which seems to offer freedom of choice but is actually limited. Binary opposition is necessary and unavoidable for reasoning, but it is a great obstacle to liberation. That is, to be truly liberated, we should stay in a composed state

---

[17] Lee, *Postmodern Ethics*, 10-11.

of mind, called "stillness" or pure "awareness" by contemporary spiritual leaders, without feeling the ego intensity in terms of anger or excitement. For sure, stillness or pure awareness is fundamentally different from the conceptually acknowledged state of being absent as opposed to being present. Nor is it some state that could be embraced by the idea of "logocentrism."

In reality, such a way of considering all beings and things with such issues as logocentrism and the ontology of being human with special intelligence over other animals, plants, and other inanimate objects quite often leads us humans to have too much pride. Such pride even causes wars with other races. The Second World War is always taken as the supreme example. Certainly, all humans in the East and West, or any continent, for that matter, are responsible for all the problems caused by our egoic desire to dominate other countries, the possibility of atomic wars, various environmental problems, global warming as a social dilemma, and unemployment. All these problems are caused by the intensity of the human ego.

2.5. The common goal of intellectuality and spirituality

In the present study, I do not want to end up only adding to academic research on truth. I would like to keep the focus of my discussion on linking intellectuality and spirituality. To directly go for something that can be shared by both academically minded scholars and general readers. On the one hand, in both East and West, considering intellectual understandings of truth has been done mainly in academic circles. On the other hand, also in both East and West, religion took the main role to plant the seriousness on the fundamental nature of humanity in people's minds. Yet it is clear to me that *the ultimate goal of intellectuality and spirituality in both East and West has been the same—to reach the most fundamental dimension of life which lies beyond thinking and language.* In a sense, the term "spirituality" seems to carry this purpose more than intellectual work, but pursuing something "spiritual," to some, might sound like blindly falling for something unreasonable and mystical.

However, I am convinced that what is truly intellectual, particularly in the field of literature and the arts, is genuinely "spiritual." By this, I mean that when we discuss what is human, the humanness essentially has to be linked to spirituality. Indeed, as it is commonly known in Ch'an/Seon/Zen Buddhism, what is genuinely real does not take its form in thinking and language, thus nor in social phenomena. It actually lies beyond thinking, which is possible as the ego function. Nonetheless, I believe that the capacity and value of the ego as the tool to be used by the real self goes beyond simply being a useless or harmful obstacle. Well used, the ego's understanding of the world and the true self present to the unmanifested true self a limitlessly vast realm of possibility to manifest itself. It cannot be dismissed that intellectual knowing takes the very important role of a guide book that directs us to the goal, helping us reach and encounter the spiritual space. Philosophy's purpose is just that. Literature and critical theory pursue the same purpose, but they do so with the power of emotion and affect in a more profound way.

Without an intellectual explanation of how we can perceive the appearance of the infinite self in the sequence of the given time and place, the meaning and activities to promote spirituality could be collapsed and used by some mystic spiritual healers. Of course, spiritual teaching and meditation can heal and make ordinary people healthier, but they cannot be used as the prime goal in a mystical way. An exact understanding of the true nature of the infinite self is necessary above all.

Yet it is a fact that the empirical intellectualization of the ego almost always sets you off the real self. It ceaselessly keeps one's mind in an unstable state. Yet we have the ability to see all objects as they are—"things-in-themselves" in Kant's terms—going beyond the ego function. In everyday life, if you see objects as they are without your ego's fabrication of their images, you will have the genuine wisdom to understand them and to better them. Without the hindrance of the ego's discernment, we would have the ability to confront the real nature of objects and phenomena as they are. The genuine meaning of spirituality comes into the picture. Spirituality is the true nature beyond the me-centered way of thinking. It is the essence of the universal that is empty of phenomena, and that is why it is called "Emptiness" in Mahayana Buddhism. In this way, intellectuality and spirituality go together.

2.6. Genuine happiness

Everyone wants to live a happy life, whatever meaning or situation "happy" may present to us. As long as we are alive, happiness is our primary interest and, in reality, the most important component of our life that makes us live with liveliness and vigor. This matter of happiness is never simple but always our most immanent concern. Happiness understood on the shallow level is opposed to unhappiness, sadness, and depression. Happiness in this mode of thought is rather the feeling of being pleased, which is the basic structure of all humans and which has been characteristically inherited in the primarily dual structure of Western thought.

At any rate, we often lose the verity of its deeper phase of happiness. In fact, the usual or superficial meaning the word presents is the feeling we obtain with sensory gratification, as in "Are you happy now with what you wanted?" or "I am happy because I got a good grade on this test." Any sensory gratification we experience in such cases is the satisfaction of the ego, our outward mindset that most immediately controls thought and behavior when in touch with external reality. When the ego faces external objects, as mentioned above, it compares its achievements with those of others. It sees objects in terms of material or mental values. To the ego, mental or material values are directly related to how much the object pleases it, especially compared to other objects. It is only the feeling of happiness as opposed to pain and suffering.

The sensibility we come to experience while meditating is not such a shallow and unstable feeling of happiness. The feeling of happiness as the opposite of sadness or unhappiness is of a dreamlike quality. One feels happy, not sad or depressed, but that happy feeling is only shallow and fleeting. The happy feeling has no depth and does not last; it is only a transient form that disappears very quickly, like sadness or unhappy feelings. Why is it so? Because it is half of the whole, of which the other half is the feeling of pain, sadness, and suffering. The two different sides are like the flipsides of a coin. Happiness and despair, pleasure and pain, and good and evil come only as pairs. However, ordinary people are unaware of the solid fact that beyond the phenomenon of the division of the two opposites, they are one, and thus no reasoning or judging is possible. The two opposites, good and evil, happiness and pain, come out of this dimension beyond phenomena—Emptiness. It is also Buddha-nature, original self, or God, Heaven, or Paradise in Christian terms.

This deeper phase of happiness or "joy," "bliss," or liberation is usually not carried through the insubstantial, commonsensical at most, understanding of happiness. True happiness does not mean the simple feeling of being gratified. It is not complicated or difficult to think that true happiness arises on a limitless ground that produces all finite phenomena. At the same time, precisely because it is all-embracing, the dimension of truth is rather separate from and beyond the ephemeral pleasures we usually experience. The deep feeling of true and lasting happiness comes to us as we comprehend and accept it—the root of short-lived gratification.

The source of genuine happiness can be termed the dimension of "pure awareness," which does not attach our mind to perceivable objects but lies behind, beneath, or beyond them all. That is to say, true happiness is never a feeling of satisfaction of the ego; in contrast, it is approachable only when the ego becomes a tool of pure awareness, which is the true, cosmic self. It is such an obvious matter that the primary quality of ultimate reality, which would make us fundamentally happy at a level deeper than phenomenal objects, must be vast—actually limitless.

But for so many who would not allow themselves to step forward, it would be too big a leap to recognize and positively accept this nature of infinity and limitlessness. To many of us who keep to such a way of thinking, I would like to propose a simple way of objectively looking through the history of Western metaphysics. If one simply takes a look at the history of Western philosophy and literature, they would realize that the Western mind has always taken such vast, actually limitless truth as its principal subject, although Western philosophers have attempted to grasp it as the identity of the supreme entity. In thinking on this subject, we do not have to be religious in the sense that we ideologically manifest faithful devotion to an acknowledged unique truth or deity attached to the belief in and reverence for a supernatural power or powers regarded as creating and governing the universe.

Whether it is the subject of an ordinary conversation or of academic writing and debates, it is quite clear that the primary quality of the ultimate reality, which would make us fundamentally happy at a level deeper than that of phenomenal objects, must be not only deep and vast but an actually limitless realm. However, it is nothing but the ultimate reality of ourselves and our world. We are not only connected to others in the same space and society living at the same time. All of us are interconnected with one another. More than that, in the innermost part, we are fundamentally one consciousness. Yet for so many who would not allow themselves to step forward, it would be too big a leap to recognize and positively accept this nature of infinity and limitlessness.

Truth/true self/God/Buddha is always with you, whatever you are, think, or do, but you are not consciously aware of its presence. It is *not* a matter of having religious faith. Being a theist or an atheist is only a matter of following religious doctrine, which is an ideology, nothing more. But we are talking about having true spirituality that lies above any kind of ideology. In other words, you can feel (not reason) your true self whenever you lower your ego power, whether through any religion or not. Dropping the ego power surely makes peace live, active peace in the middle of everyday life and relationships with others.

Genuinely spiritual happiness should bring pure awareness, which should not be conceived of only as a strictly academic subject. However, it can never be dismissed as an unproven and mystic matter. A deep sense of happiness as the most significant component of our life is essentially unthinkable if it is thought of without a connection to pure awareness.

Unfortunately, many are simply led by so-called "naturally" occurring thoughts and emotions, and they feel too busy to concern themselves with genuine happiness and spirituality. They simply pursue what pleases them. When they are sensuously gratified, whether alone, with their family, or in other ways, they say they are happy. They forget that happy feelings can bring a narrow view of life, and they lose chances to have a broader vision that embraces the other side of what they like, love, and enjoy. All these emotions go together with the *reasoning* mind. As a result, when they think about or confront what they do not like, love, or enjoy, those who do not take the spiritual depth of life seriously feel unhappiness and get stressed.

No doubt, people who understand that the two issues—the feelings of happiness and deeper gratification—come with purity of the mind are broad-minded. They may even be accustomed to inner stillness through meditation by calming down, looking into their own mind, and rediscovering that the self is not the ego that consists of fragmented ideas but pure awareness of the whole. The whole means the entirety of humanity, or, as Carl Gustav Jung called it, "the collective unconscious." His psychological term was "unconscious" in that we humans do not know it, but it is obviously pure consciousness and aware of the whole. It means that we would also go on to advance the state of collective humanity in this way so as to reduce the danger of social conflict and international war. This is not a coward's way of shunning the reality of society and the world. In contrast to misapprehension, relying on the true self will bring you not only peace and happiness but a more peaceful world, one where we all share the results of scientific, technological, and spiritual advances.

It is important to realize that truly pure awareness is not the form of a one-sided mind that only embraces the other. It is a mind that truly lies beyond the concepts of purity and impurity: that is, it is the fundamental spiritual power, which takes form in both purity and impurity, good and evil, right and wrong, and, ultimately, presence and absence. It has *complete freedom to choose or deny either of the poles*. Genuinely pure awareness is the state of liberation from the ego and is thus unbound by the condition of sense perception and thought. In fact, pure awareness is the center of the mind.

At the center of your being, your true self is in itself free from perception, concept, and memory and constantly experiences, which is the fountain of true, fundamental wisdom. When you are in the habit of calming down and keeping composure with meditation, you will find that your life is filled more and more with inner peace, genuine happiness, and fundamental joy and that your ego will lose the power of anger, folly, and foolish desires for sensuous pleasures. Simply put, you will see everything fall into place.

As Mevlâna Jalâluddîn Rumi (1207-1273), the leader and great poet of Islam, has said, only stillness is the language of God, a language that carries the meaning of one's true self, and all else is poor translation. Stillness should be the unconditioned state beyond the meaning of no sound and no movement. It is vital that stillness means no excessive and adhesive thinking generated by the ego. "Be still and know that I am God" (Ps. 46:10) also means "Be still and know that you are God," who is in you as your true self. God and you are not in an object-subject relation. The infinite Truth and you are just one. That is to say, God and you see each other with the same eyes—there is only "seeing" and no different seers.

2.7. The necessary part of the ego and excessive intensity

Ego as the power of thinking must be a vehicle that carries your true, universal self. You should realize that your true self is not the petty, whimsical ego that is easily attached to the transient appearances of phenomena happening to you or around you. The purpose of thinking should just be clearly understanding phenomena as they are. More than that proper role, the ego is like a mass of good and bad emotions that seems to want to destroy others for its own survival and interest. But ultimately, it is destructible to itself. Your ego is mischievous and cunning, and it will keep transforming into the power of positive thinking and creations in life, disguising itself as your true self. Thus, your ego's work must be checked down to be the power of healthy and smart choices.

The goal of practicing to be in a superior meditative state of mind is to remove the unwholesome ego power. The ego wishes to live a special life and feel superior to others. After all, the universal infinite self reflects itself onto your personality as the mirror. The vast, universal self which lives beyond time and space cannot be reflected from the mirror, your false self. Therefore, except for its power for healthy, clear, and smart judgment, the ego has to be abolished. In other words, the intensity of the ego has to give way. Thus, I am by no means willing to say that the ego as the power of thinking is entirely useless and self-destructive. Still, as the form of the self, the ego plays an extremely significant role in our lives, but in a sense, it should be treated as a raw material like money, and it can be a great source of power for one's life and others.

The first key to unlocking genuine happiness is surrendering the ego to the world in front of you, which might not seem to make sense at first. Yet you have to remember that the space of what is totally other than the world of egoic thinking is always there in you. As you look inside the situation without egoic greed, you will see almost all is actually positive. At any rate, it is the form of one's mind itself that shows one's personality and deep wishes. Despite the fact that the ego is an illusion and has no actual power, I propose we ought not to consider it as worthless and harmful only. It works as the self insofar as we live, and we should know what it is and how it works. Our task is to employ its structure or frame, not low-quality emotions, as the tool to be used by the real self. The structure of the ego without its intensity to attach a value to an object is necessary precisely because ultimately everything is done with judgment, linguistic expression, thinking, and behavior. We should live as the real self in the form of the ego. We as light live in a world of egos, but to bind the whole of it to that value is an excessive and valueless power attachment that is harmful to it. That is, we live in so many relations to others through the fundamentality of that relation, that is love as true Emptiness, not the egoic feeling of gratifying its need by helping others. In order to practice love and compassion for others, we should embrace the world in itself, filled with other egos, with the form of our ego. We should face the world with love and compassion and without hatred and jealousy, but we should have a view of the world through the outward form of the imaginary and the symbolic in terms of Jacques Lacan's theory of psychoanalysis.

That is the goal of sermons, centering prayer, and meditation, which direct the practitioner's mental gaze inward and keep a meditative state of mind in everyday life. Reducing stress and becoming wiser are surely the expected fruits. Yet, to put it in a larger context, the goal is to reduce the power of the self-conflicting ego. The self-conflict is due to its nature to attach objects, whether outside or inside, and eventually to abolish the entire ego intensity, leaving only the frame. As one reaches the point of abolishing the ego, one attains "awakening" or "enlightenment," as Buddhists call it. It is waking up from a dream that is none other than this life. The influence of spiritual leaders on the modern world is not limited to stress reduction. Its final goal is to let people attain awakening from wanton thoughts, which are essentially delusions. In a similar manner, the real nature of the end of literature and the arts should also be enlightenment, as in Buddhism, or spiritual maturity to be near enlightenment, to say the least. It is a full breakthrough to another dimension of mind, which is the Buddha-mind—a mind of unconditional love and perfect compassion. We must not think that awakening is only a Buddhist concept. In the Christian religion, it surely is attaining Jesus Christ's mind or becoming filled with God's Holy Spirit.

Is there a firm distinction between the true self with the ability to love others and do the right things wisely and the egoic mind which distorts such a peaceful state of mind? Is it possible for us to switch over from the egoic mind to the true self and live like it? It is possible, beyond doubt. The ego is a false self separated from the fundamental, real one, and it identifies itself by comparing itself with others and thus by feeling superiority, inferiority, or mediocre. However, because it is not the real, constant self, it disappears as it is watched. As prominent and believable Buddhist and secular spiritual leaders declare, the ego as an individual consciousness does not really exist with substance. It only lasts for some time in some place, but there is no way of measuring the length of time or the solid ground of the space upon which the I is situated. If we want to enjoy deep happiness and receive the benefits of spirituality, we are supposed to abandon the ego that grows and feels happy and loving sometimes and, at other times, falls and feels sad or becomes mean, offensive, vulgar, jealous, hateful, or too weak and contracted. The ego is childish, immature, and quite often turns out to be vile or cowardly toward the objects in the world, which ultimately means toward itself, the source of that thinking.

The ego is whimsical and irresponsible because it lacks the power to stand in the middle between the polar opposites—this point and that. The middle does not phenomenally appear to the mind's eye, let alone the physical eyes, so it is a blind spot, and it can easily become an unnecessary obstacle when the ego finds itself stuck in between two choices and feels uncomfortable. The ego is confused and lost between two objects of its desire. It oscillates between the two, trying to know what is more profitable to itself. Desire strengthens the illusory nature of the ego. However, the ego does not know that the objects of its desire, itself included, are transient and only experience fleeting moments. It relies only on tangible objects and does not accept the nature of the undecidable itself, while in the ultimate reality, there is nothing stable with a fixed and everlasting essential quality. Because the nature of the ego is the tenacity to show up and cling to objects with avarice and despise the objects it hates, it is very difficult, almost impossible, for it to calm down and see objects in themselves. It always compares itself and what it does with others and what others do. The natural result is that one becomes either arrogant with self-conceit and looks down upon others or despairs of success and loses hope. Ultimately, the ego only has to be the form of the psyche and mind, and it has to give way to the true self for the sake of itself, which is one's mental and corporeal life. The ego power alone that takes its identity only from external objects does not care for its real nature and ruins itself.

The ego does not leave when you hate it and try to remove it from your mind, so innumerable kinds of thought become ingrained and overwhelm you. The ego leaves when you show it openness and compassion, but with a strict coldness and nonchalance. You have to show sympathy and compassion to your ego, but at the same time you ought to be callous and insensible to it with no concern. Sitting meditation is the most effective way of converting the mind to the deepest, purest state of mind and start living practicing loving kindness. Walking meditation and various other additional kinds of meditations also help practitioners. The ego leaves while it is watched over by the real self. Facing the light, the darkness goes away, and you find yourself in a state of clear-mindedness and joy without suffering anxiety. As you spend more and more time in the no egoic thought zone, the way you think and express yourself will truly change.

The ego is the self-image constructed in the early stages of life, between 6 and 18 months, according to Lacan, whose psychoanalytic theory is celebrated worldwide in late 20th- and early 21st-century literary criticism. The ego is what thinks of itself as "I am," and it surely lasts to the end of one's life. What thinks of itself as "I am" is nothing but a system of hardened ideas that comprise oneself. It offers one a very narrow view of oneself and of the world one sees. The ego only wants to be pleased and happy, but it is whimsical and changes the objects of its desires one after another; its desire has no end. Its primary principle is having pleasure, and that is why Sigmund Freud started his psychoanalysis with the concept of the "pleasure principle." When its instinctual impulses to attain immediate pleasure are not satisfied, it feels sad, fear, anxious, or angry, and it bullies others and also turns against itself. It usually compares itself and what it has with others and what they have. It turns out to be too proud and then lacks self-esteem. This way, it constantly experiences love as the feelings of attachment and hate, its opposite, happiness and depression. It absolutely lacks the ability to love others unconditionally. When it feels that it loves others, it does so for the sake of its interest. Egoic love is to satisfy its own desire. It goes on to the point of torturing itself and even of committing suicide.

Therefore, this nature of the ego reveals that it is a store and mechanism of avarice and greed. The ego is the self that one has as one lives a life, but it is separate from the real source of life and is formed in the early (mirror) stages of life. That is, the ego is a fabricated, false self like a mask. It is neither my nor anyone else's idea that it is so; it is nothing but a fact. It fabricates situations not only in favorable but also unfavorable ways for itself. The ego makes you feel overtly proud of yourself, but it will also make you feel a victim of circumstance, burdened, irresponsible, and trapped.

In Christianity, Jesus Christ is called the "Son of God," but he went through suffering and tests and succeeded in overcoming the desire of his egoic individual self. It is a fact that he could not help but get angry and cleanse the temple by overturning the tables of money changers and sellers of objects of sacrifice without perfect wisdom and discernment (Matt.

21:12-13). It is not the ego intensity but its frame with the slightest phenomenality of the ego. Jesus shows fear as he realizes his death is coming. He asks God to take his death on the cross away from him, but he prays, "Yet not My will, but Yours be done" (Luke 22:42). His attachment to human life is shown even during his last breath: "My God, My God, why have you forsaken Me?" (Matt. 27:46). Jesus is saying so as a human, with the unavoidable remnant of his egoic nature.

The great religious figures are the supreme examples of those who lived without ego intensity. The archetypes would surely be the first leaders such as Jesus Christ and Shakyamuni Buddha on whose teachings the main religions emerged. Both went through intensive self-training to abolish their ego and reach enlightenment. Gautama Buddha was a prince and had everything the usual secular people desired at his disposal—power, wealth, living in a magnificent palace, a loving wife, and a beloved son. He left all these behind and went far away, seeking truth. He attained enlightenment, which was the awakening from the dream context of life. He was sure he overcame life's problems of birth, aging, sickness, and death. Without question, it is not that he gained the miraculous power of not aging, not becoming ill, and not dying. He reached the moment of awakening by dropping the whole of his ego intensity. Yet he still had the discerning power of reason and emotion that can be identified as the minimal phenomenality of being limited in time and space. People from all walks of life came to him and became his disciples—from royalty to those of the lowest class. He had great wisdom to teach them in the best way for each individual, treating them all on an equal basis.

In this light, reading and watching films lead us to infinity, which does not allow itself to be revealed by our reasoning capacity that goes within the domain of time and space. Yet behind reason and phenomena, the ultimate reality infinitely creates all movements and phenomena through binary opposition, which is the essence of movement. The ultimate reality is the spirituality that embraces the whole and freely uses rationality when thinking is needed. At the end of the day, being is already doing. Being is already a curious, mysterious, abstruse movement. That is how we can say that God is the most fundamental love who embraces both good and evil.

That is to say, literature and films offer us precious opportunities to experience true happiness and unconditional love, reaching a spiritually awakened state of mind. The true happiness we all want is not the simple feeling of being gratified. Non-duality does not mean one. In Mahayana Buddhism, non-duality indicates "not one, but not two." This "not one, but not two" describes the undecidability of the relation between the I and the other, transcendence and phenomena, the infinite true self and the finite ego.

It is the quality of the entire exterior of the ego, the thinking mind, truly in oneness beyond and within phenomena. In reading literary works or watching movies, "the sublime" is the most profound and nuclear stage through which we approach non-duality, as I will elaborate on in the next chapter.

CHAPTER THREE

LITERARY TEXTS AND FILMS
AS VAST *KONGANS*

3.1. Literature and film lead us to encounter pure consciousness

When it comes to the issue of spiritual practices, meditation in particular, we should not restrict our view to some specific styles of religious or secular meditation. I regard America now as a privileged place on this point. Most Americans who are interested in spirituality—whether religious or not—are very pure-minded and sincere. One of the great merits of their society of spirituality in general, and Buddhism in particular, is not so much that it is systematic, but rather that it is out of the grasp of corruption. We see that other major religions become corrupt when they become too systematic and come to have too much social power. To me, it is clear that the novelty and purity of American Buddhism is a great merit. American Buddhist society is, at least in the present age, an exemplary one for the world. When I attend meditation sessions and retreats, I see Americans' earnestness to be more spiritual.

I started attending a Buddhist meditation group meeting at a Presbyterian church! I do not think it is simply a matter of the economic situation of the church. I found later that the pastor was open-minded to other religions. You would not see such a phenomenon in other countries where there are systematic conservative religions with strong systems. Conservative believers stick to systematic dogmas that set up strict or even stubborn rules. The leaders of different religions or different sects in one religion compete against each other to have stronger political and social power. One of the characteristics of American Buddhism is that many leaders and meditation teachers are lay people rather than clergy, such as ministers and monks.

We usually see that, in other countries, people of religion are ministers. It is an undeniable fact that innumerable pure-minded religious people in the world find consolation in their religions and seek peaceful lives by practicing morality. However, it is also true that religious leaders become dishonest with their believers and depend upon egoic conflicts to enlarge their systems and sects. Administrative ministers are so addicted to power in their social systems that they do not even know the fact that they are. From a spiritual aspect, they are just going blind.

In contrast, Western secular spiritual societies—especially in America, Canada, and Britain—make fresh and wonderful examples. I sincerely hope that the secular ways of the spiritual societies of non-duality will influence the rest of the world. The greatest merit I would like to emphasize is that the representative spiritual teachers such as Eckhart Tolle, Adyashanti, Wilber, and Jack Kornfield use Buddhism as the main basis for their teachings of non-dual spirituality and the path to awakening to pure consciousness. They also very often make use of phrases or stories in the Christian Bible (especially Jesus's words in the four Gospels), a Taoist Sutra like *Tao-te Ching,* the poems of Rumi, a Sufi Muslim (Sufism is a form, rather than a sect, of mysticism in Islam), and the teachings of Ramana Maharshi and other Indian spiritual leaders.[18] I want to express my admiration for the ways of liberal spiritual societies. What has most impressed me over the years is the fact that American Buddhist meditation practitioners talk about Jesus Christ and the leaders of Islam and Hinduism.

Now, I would like to make a sincere suggestion for the spiritual societies of the US and the rest of the world. Let us now start to talk more concretely about how we can practice meditation without the heavy feeling that we "have to do" something. We really do not need training or practice to become calm and have wisdom for a spiritual life. In fact, I believe that the American *free,* not conservative, way of thinking is the best way of questing for true spirituality, since spirituality is perfect freedom from our corporal reality. Yet it is noticeable that perfect freedom does not mean we avoid a physical and social life. It rather means that spirituality is not, as is simply understood, purely mental.

In fact, we can practice meditation in every moment of our daily lives. When learning at school, busily working, or engaging in other parts of everyday life, you face easy, uneasy, or difficult phases in which it is hard to bring together unconditioned pure awareness and intellectuality formed first with sense perception. In *true* reality, for spiritual life, you do not have to feel the burden of "doing something for yourself." I remember that I could not even start meditating when I was young. I was a junior high school student, and I tried to sit in the Buddha posture. I failed to assume that

---

[18] Tolle took his first name, Eckhart, from Meister Eckhart, the name of a 13th-century German Christian theologian and mystic. Jacques Derrida favored Meister Eckhart's negative (Apophatic) theology, a form of theology that approaches God by negating all characteristics that do not belong to God.

position, and I felt I could not begin meditating at all. I now think it was an entirely awkward situation, and I do think that the authors of such books and other strict meditation teachers are simply out of date. Today we live in a postmodern era.

I should like to say that in such open social and cultural environments, especially powerful areas to advance our spirituality in everyday life are literature, film, and other art forms. *Literature, film, and other arts are special areas that lead audiences outside the local, petty ego—that is to say, into the dimension of the true self or the Transmiddle Zone with the special power of sensibility.*

Whether it is intended or unintended by the literary authors and other artistic creators, the innate goal of deconstructing (to put it in a more understandable way, destroying the structure of) the binary structure is itself reaching beyond human thinking capacity. Film is certainly different from literature in many ways, but both literature and film engage our intellectuality (reasoning and deep thinking) and our feelings, mainly regarding stories and subjects that inspire discussion with different opinions. Other art forms appeal mainly to an audience's emotions.

Literature and film offer us opportunities to explore pure consciousness through concrete life stories and everyday affairs. They are entirely unlike traditional philosophy or religious sermons. If you experience spirituality as pure consciousness that lies beyond or right at the core of your being, you will find your way to the ultimate reality in whatever you do. I think that great works of literature and film have more potential to usher us to the gate of true spirituality than the conventional teachings of religions as the systems that drive us to a religious doctrine. A religious doctrine is an ideology; it is generated as a set of ideas and beliefs. Literature and film mostly consist of the protagonists' extreme suffering, great failures, unsolved answers, and even their and/or others' deaths. Thus, it is possible that literature and film at first do not seem to be special devices to calm yourself down as sitting or walking meditation do. Among the many art forms, literature and film stimulate our imagination so that we may glimpse the ultimate reality that lies in the deepest part of our being. The ultimate reality is beyond the sequence of past, present, and future, and the door to it is "here and now." Literature and film lead us to this door by destroying the illusory binary structure of life through ambiguity.

Most people do not focus their attention on *perfect* emptiness (which I describe as "Emptiness") that lies behind the transient, illusory vision of the here and now, which is a passing phenomenon. For them, it is emptiness that is no more than non-existence. What I mean by Emptiness in this book is not simply a lack of the concept of being that is called non-being.

Emptiness has no room for the concepts of being or non-being. Nor do they seem to usher you to the Transmiddle Zone in the sense that you are free to choose either side.

Let us enter into a slightly more serious discussion of time and space because literature and film lead us to glimpses of the ultimate reality, which lies beyond time and space. How long is the "now"? One century? Ten years? One minute? One second? Film washes over us at 24 frames per second. Still, how long is now? Is there any flow of time to be called "now"? I do not think so. I would never say there is any period of a stream of time that could be called "now." We might also think more deeply about the concept of "here" or space. How broad or wide is "here"? Clearly, the so-called "now" or "here" cannot be measured. I do not mean that we just live moment by moment until our last breath and disappear. At each moment, the dimension of Emptiness where there is no irony of phenomena reveals itself to us, although there is no way of measuring it. I mean, in the deepest part of the very presence, here and now, we as one spirit manifest in everything throughout the whole world and universe.

I would like to call this presence of the middle of here and now "appearing as disappearing." It is *not* right, or at least not precise, to say that a phenomenon appears and then disappears after a while. "A moment" is the result of the conceptualization of a very short passage of time of existence that is identified with our feeling and thinking. However, the conceptualization of the time flow is possible only when we forget what is really happening in that short period and assume that it is OK for us to think that what seems to be happening or to have happened lasts. Let us look into the details of what we think is taking place there. We know that a motion picture needs 24 frames per second in order to present movement. Nevertheless, if we look into what really happens, we would know that there is nothing that really divides time. We can divide one second into a thousand or infinitely more divisions.

This proves that a length of time is due to our attachment to consciously knowing what is happening. I would like to claim that in the ultimate reality, or perfect emptiness itself, *a phenomenon appears as it really disappears.* By this, I mean that we can never find out how long a state stays fixed. There is no length of the unmoving, stable state. As a thing appears to our perceiving mind, it does so by disappearing. The other side of appearance is disappearance. In this sense, strictly speaking, it is not right to say that a thing "comes into being" since being already and only means non-being. Thus, the whole process of existence is a dream context. Existing in the world is like a dream. Isn't it so? A literary story is also in a dream context.

While literature does it without set images that would direct our minds, film, a genre of popular art, offers us an optical vision on the screen. Films do not open our minds to the world of individual imagination as much as literature does. Yet a film has the power to present an opportunity to have insight into what is important for life within a short running time. It does so with the mass entertainment values that we can confront in our daily lives. Therefore, it is very easy for the public to fall for the side of easily understood fantasy and fun that are presented to them through themes and messages. Yet films also have the power to draw the public's attention beyond the possible themes of the story, images, and sound through various cinematic techniques.

Literature and film might at first arouse your emotions and stimulate logical reasoning. However, later, you may find that they have led you to the profound depths of your mind through narratives, moving images, and sound. At least, this will be your experience according to critics who unite intellectuality and spirituality. Such criticism reveals that we are all in the ultimate truth as *one* beyond the sequence of time and space.

To be sure, "God," "the wholly Other," "the Real," "the real I," "the true self," "the whole," and "the One" are all different names for the same dimension that is pre-linguistic and unlimited by time and space. It is the infinitely expansive and single, universal mind. Jesus Christ employs symbols, metaphors, and stories that draw us and point us to the ultimate reality, which is the Kingdom of Heaven or Christ's consciousness. Christ's consciousness is the fountain of our mind through which God's creation constantly continues by conditioning all phenomena. We would spiritually experience God's radiant living word with the most vivid way of describing it with symbols, metaphors, and anecdotes.

It is now high time for us to find the source of life and live as it! In order to do this, we should truly comprehend and accept the fact that, through symbols and metaphors, poems, films, or stories, whether short or long, *break the shell of our ego—the structure of binary opposition.* Of course, the story of a novel or a film as a work of art is much longer than the parables Jesus used. After all, a novel or film introduces us to the ultimate reality of our life.

The great works of literature and film direct our attention outside the ordinary habit of the ego. There is one more step toward the right comprehension of literature, film, and other arts. More than Jesus' parables, the prominent literary texts comprise tragic and/or Gothic stories and conclusions that depict Emptiness. As a very easy example, while the ego wants to feel satisfied and happy, almost if not all of the masterpieces do not present the audiences with satisfying endings as their separate and changing egos primarily want. The theme of a story takes a tangible form in the given society, but the ultimate aim of the linguistic work of art in itself shows how the ego of the protagonist fails to flourish in society, and they instead are led to open their mind outside the ego. In this way, film versions of great literary works and prominent films in themselves attract wide audiences with entertaining worth.

From this perspective, the fundamental, prime goal of reading a story or watching a great movie is to obtain deep insight into Emptiness and reach the foundation of genuine wisdom for living itself. The story and mood determine the thoughts and feelings you experience, and as you are immersed in the story and sound, so *the space of pure consciousness emerges and enlarges*. Your awareness of the ultimate reality will surely grow as your experiences of appreciating literary and cinematic masterpieces and great works of other arts—such as paintings and music—accumulate.

The attractive and affective power of a film derives from the associated images on the screen and sounds. Despite the fact that they are different arts, literature and film share the same goal of finding and encountering the most profound spirituality of ourselves. The point I should like to emphasize is that critical theory should serve the audience in this light. Criticism and theory should serve readers by explaining how literary texts and films work. This chapter presents in more detail how literary reading and watching movies work as a meditation technique.

Prior to the main discussion of literature and film, let us first go to the value of symbols and metaphors that nearly all readers will know. A supreme example would be Jesus Christ's teachings in the New Testament. Jesus describes the Kingdom of Heaven, an *imperceptible and ineffable* spiritual dimension, not by using "sacred" or theological words but by consistently using simple images, similes, symbols, and analogies. He uses such expressions as the Kingdom of God is "like" so and so. His open secret can be understood through the fundamental attunement of the heart for pure, unconditional love. He makes himself clear: "Do you think I am talking about bread? … You still don't get the point, do you? Though you have ears, you still don't hear; though you have eyes, you still don't see!" (Mark 8:17-18).

Here, Jesus shows a different style of viewing the ultimate truth rather than the commonsensical way of judgment. He is saying that his disciples do not yet know that the best way to talk about spiritual transcendence is through metaphors! Jesus does not show us a way of explaining the Kingdom of Heaven in a philosophical way in order to be understood or doctrinal, for example, by saying that you must believe that God's Kingdom is the most divine dimension without heretical thought. This *inner* experience of the story recorded in the New Testament on how Jesus taught is *open beyond literalistic reading*. The metaphorical way of explaining comprises a short story, which is the same as a literary story. In other words, the final and full meaning of the Word of *True* God does not depend upon the moral "authority" (to order people with do's and don'ts) that lies in ancient religious texts.

I do think that the Christian Bible should have been interpreted in a wholly different way than the classic, conservative one and that it must be particularly for us, the citizens of the world. This is not to imply that the Bible consists of lies or visions of a fantasy world. Nonetheless, I am more than certain that Christianity, the largest religion in the world, should have led people in the right direction to the *real* God/Truth. It must lead them, at least from now on, in the postmodern age, to the *truly infinite* God. "Omniscient" and "omnipresent" infinity cannot be thought of—cannot be conceptualized—as being conditioned in time and space. Let us simply think about it: God must not be primarily a concept for obtaining money or fame. God must be for the very fundamentality of whatever it is for humanity and even inhumanity. God is the Creator of everything, and His Creation is going on right now! God has no beginning and end, and we are manifestations of God.

All genres of literature in general, and poetry in particular, employ symbolic language. Novels and dramas, although full of plain language we use every day, are also symbolic of the true reality beyond culture, history, and time. Literature, the art of language, unveils the ego through the storyline and mood. The unveiling process is the way in which it unlocks our spiritual sight. The primal reality of the ego is that it is split into two and is thus fundamentally unstable. The instability comprises "binary opposition," the basic form of the ego and its vision of the world—subject and object, good and bad, superiority and inferiority. We have not only explored this self-contradictory nature in the previous chapters but will also investigate later how literary texts and Hollywood science fiction films such as *The Matrix* (1999) reveal it to us. In a strict sense, the mechanical function of the film's matrix indicates the nature of the egoic mental construct as a false identity.

3.2. A new direction for your critical view: Experiencing the sublime

Without question, paintings, music, and other arts are included in our discussion, yet I do not intend to expand our discussion to these other arts. The primary focus of our discussion is laid on literature and film, and it will be applied to other arts as well. There are essentially two different ways to think about what literature is all about, as we would learn if we went through the long history of literature and the arts.

First, it is a common concept that reading a literary work, be it a novel or a poem, guides you, the reader, to experience another person's unconventional, eccentric story. It is commonsensically approved and goes without question, you accept profound meanings from a given literary work, and you might agree with the author's view of life with some head nodding. In this case, words are important simply because they carry "meanings" on the intellectual level. The goal of the literary work might seem to offer you thoughts and ideology, and thus to draw consent from you for the ideas in phrases, sentences, paragraphs, chapters, and eventually the whole story.

This account would seem to magnify the importance of the "meaning" that language produces, nothing more than that. In this traditional narrow view, the value of a literary work is decided by the critics and public who estimate it in a thematic approach. Some of them have an unswerving belief that literature and film must have moral, educational themes. The theme of the given piece of writing can be defined as what the work seems to the critic/reader to be. In short, it is an idea or point that appears to be central to a story. Typical examples of themes of this type are love, hatred, fear, anxiety, shock, and a general sense of conflict, whether between individuals or societies, between countries, between humans and machines, or concerning future technology that could control humans, and the dangers of unchecked ambition regarding this matter.

Of course, we can admit that thematic values are good to educate children, but beyond the line of a certain age and society, it is impossible to say what moral standards are good or bad for other societies of different ages. When the supreme leader of a nation exercises authority on literature, film, and other forms of arts and cultural situations, they are called a dictator and their government a dictatorship. Such a political situation persecutes the freedom of speech. We have seen many cases of this folly all over the world and throughout human history—mainly through wars.

From this point of view, to have a deeper vision of humanity and the world, we should try to see deep into the fundamental purpose of literary art to free humanity. A thematic approach to the work of art that is generally passed as the standard way of judging literary texts and films in itself goes against the spiritual freedom of humanity. The theme actually works like a *dictator's* message for his followers.

Let us examine what a theme really is in more detail. A theme is the subject or main idea that is supposed to complete the given literary writing or film. Yes, I agree with postmodern ethicist thought, in line with the core of Mahayana Buddhism and postmodern Christian insight. It is clear to me that a theme cannot prove its own value simply because it is a subjective abstraction and unable to embrace other possible themes. A theme is what seems to a reader to be the "main idea" that conditions the whole story with different concepts that build each part of the narration. Yet in actuality, the main idea of the work depends on the reader. The reader's personality has been formed and nurtured in the society and culture they grew up with. Hence, the production of the theme or the interpretation of the whole work relies on the cultural characteristics of the society or the individual personality.

The cultural characteristics of the society or the individual personality determine the theme of the work, and this means that the theme deprives the narration of the freedom to be interpreted in other possible ways, thus eventually concealing the way to the ultimate reality. As the theme is set up, other readers follow it, and it becomes the ground on which all images arise and fall. However, the thematic approach alone cannot lead us to the ultimate reality, which is the genuine certainty of the life of every one of us and all other animate and inanimate beings. I am convinced that literary works and films point to it as the realm out of the reach of our capacity of knowing. The clearer the theme is, the darker the way toward the exterior, the absolute beyond the circuit of the usual ego.

The core of literature, film, and other arts is the sublime experience, through which we come to glimpse the non-dual *Transmiddle* Path. In the West, the most historic thinker on the aesthetic sublime, the passageway from the ontological nature of art to spirituality, is Kant. One might call Kant the Buddha figure of the West. Kant says that pain, shock, and terror give rise to the sublime that exceeds any standard of the finite senses.[19] He goes on to say that it is possible for us to experience the subjective feeling of being one with the whole universe in itself. Jean-Luc Nancy, one of the most prominent thinkers alive, emphasizes the nature of infinity and spirituality of the feeling of the sublime in his paper "The Sublime Offering." It is sensibility that realizes the infinite—"beyond the maximum."[20] Beyond any doubt, great literary texts and films offer us a glimpse of this dimension of infinity. I will elaborate on the sublime in *Hamlet* and *Moby-Dick* in Chapter Four and in *The Strange Case of Dr. Jekyll and Mr. Hyde*

---

[19] Immanuel Kant, *Critique of Judgment*, trans. Werner S. Pluhar. (Indianapolis: Hackett Publishing Company, Inc., 1987), 106. This is Kant's third critique after *Critique of Pure Reason* and *Critique of Practical Reason*.

[20] Jean-Luc Nancy, "The Sublime Offering," in *Of the Sublime: Presence in Question*, ed. Rodolphe Gasche and Mark C. Taylor, trans. Jeffrey S. Librett (Albany: State University of New York Press, 1993), 25-53.

and *The Picture of Dorian Gray* in Chapter Five. Here, I would like to practically demonstrate how those supreme examples have the great power to offer the reader the motives of the sublime aesthetic experience.

Although prominent Western thinkers like Kant did not know Buddhism, their insight into the most profound depths of life corresponds to Buddhist philosophy. Buddhism as a whole shows that the form of every being and every thing appears and disappears essentially in the dimension of Emptiness, in which nature never belongs either to the concept of presence or that of absence. From this point of view, it is right to say that the sublime is a mental state that is like a weak *Samadhi*. *Samadhi* is a Buddhist term for the powerful meditative state of high-level concentration. Emptiness and *Samadhi* should not be misunderstood in the sense of nihilistic nothingness as many, including even such great Western thinkers as Nietzsche and Heidegger, did. In contrast, Emptiness is beyond the identities of presence and absence, movement and stability, optimism and nihilism. It does not include a concept or feeling of nihilism. So should the sublime be understood. Tragedies and Gothic fiction do not mean to drive readers to a negative view of life. The sublime experience steers our ordinary feelings to their fading state.

Samadhi, in the Mahayana Buddhism of Northern Asian countries, or *Jhana*, in the Theravada Buddhism of South Asian countries, is the highly pure spiritual state that is the passage to Emptiness, which language cannot reach. The notion of *Samadhi* is comparable with the Western concept of the sublime, the spiritually heightened state of aesthetic feeling. I am convinced that the mental state that can be called *Samadhi*, or at least *quasi-Samadhi*, has constantly been explored in the studies of Western literature and the arts. The sensibility of the sublime has been considered to transcend ordinary, empirical feelings. This experience is fundamentally the same kind of sensibility as *Samadhi* or *Jhana*.

In this light, the ultimate goals of sublime aesthetic sensibility and Buddhist meditation are the same. By reading literary works and watching films in a manner of deconstructing binary opposition, we may stop excessive thinking and experience the ultimate reality of daily life through *Samadhi*.

3.3. A literary text or a film as a *kongan*

The main purpose of fine arts and music is to arouse our feelings so that our imaginative capacity is unlocked. Compared to those arts, literature as the art of language has two ways of activating our imagination—through our feelings and our reasoning faculty. It is ingenious, accurate, and surprisingly wise to say that literature "is a privileged ground for the realization of emptiness."[21] Novels, poems, and dramas are excellent ways for readers to become interested, intrigued, and deeply motivated to be awakened from the ego's fundamental *illusion* that the outside "objective" reality is truly real. Literature works just like Buddhist *kongans*—a very short story that raises a rigid irony and shows no reasonable solution to the irony set in the given context.

Very briefly, *kongans* and *hwadus* are the anecdotes and keywords that lead Ch'an and Seon meditation practitioners beyond language and thought. A *kongan* is a nonsensical and ironic story, while a *hwadu* is a very laconic question that sums up the *kongan* and has a complex meaning. *Kongans* and *hwadus* are meaningless when interpreted with the power of the egoic brain function. The Korean word "*ghanhwa-seon*" can be translated as "keyword/phrase/sentence-guided meditation" or simply as "keyword meditation." This means "keen observation (*ghan*) of the *hwadu*." Keyword meditation shows us what the final goal of Buddhist meditation is. The most exemplary question used in this meditation is, "What is this (that makes me think/drags my body)?" The practitioner must experience *kongans* and *hwadus* without any intention to do anything else than have the pure desire to reach the true reality beyond reason and emotion. As I elaborated in *Postmodern Ethics, Emptiness, and Literature,* the characteristic of literature and the arts is that it "pave ways for the self of the reader to escape the binary opposition and have a universal consciousness."[22]

I will be explaining here, in an easily understandable way rather than in academic terms, how we can enter the inner state of our fundamental nature, similar to *Samadhi,* that is, how we can take at least a *glimpse* of the *non-dual* and therefore *universal* mind by reading a literary text or watching a film. It is a way of going beyond the polar opposites of the basic frame of the ego, the matrix of all sorts of emotions—from happiness to pain—which are necessary for a decision-making system. The sublime takes place at the end of the story where the opposites are destroyed. The sublime is the aesthetic momentum through which readers or viewers experience a breakthrough to that inner space of *non-duality*. In the space of non-duality, everything and anything is *"not one, but not two."*

I would like to explore infinity as the goal of the sublime as we examine Vipassana meditation and Ch'an/Seon meditation as well as Western postmodern ethics. After all, these aesthetic, religious, and philosophical issues are ways of reaching the fountain of genuine wisdom, love, and

---

[21] Jeff Humphries, *Reading Emptiness: Buddhism and Literature* (Albany: State University of New York Press, 1999), 45.

[22] Lee, *Postmodern Ethics*, 10.

happiness. Accepting what is taking place in itself is observing it from the viewpoint of *Bhodhi*, the true wisdom that lies beyond the phenomenon of binary opposition. Yet it is not simply the middle zone between the polar opposites that forms a binary opposition. We can reach the realm of true wisdom as we *deconstruct* the binary opposition by accepting and excluding both, and genuine wisdom comes with the sublime feeling. Only by examining how a literary work or film accepts and excludes the opposites—that is, builds and deconstructs at the same time—can we truly be released from the constraint of the enigmatic mystery of life's problems and the pains we go through.

All these thoughts in postmodern critical theory or Buddhist traditions share the same point that valuable wisdom comes not from within but from the exterior of the ego. This spirituality is what the reader comes to attain while reading. I believe that this is *not* a difficult issue for *general readers*. In the next chapters, where I will demonstrate how to appreciate literary works and films, I will be trying to employ *plain, easily comprehensible language for general readers.*

The aesthetic effect of the sublime that a literary reader or a film viewer experiences will not be as strong as the moment of sudden enlightenment in Buddhism, a moment of genuine spirituality. Nonetheless, the impacts of the different kinds of experiences are of the same nature, in the sense that the sublime undoubtedly leads the reader or viewer beyond phenomenal language, which is formed with reasoning thoughts and ordinary emotions. The concepts sunder in your mind as you experience the sublime. This experience of the sublime belongs to the Buddhist doctrine of *sudden awakening,* which fits the description of the vision of spiritual enlightenment in the *Avatamsaka Sutra,* rather than that of gradual cultivation with learning.

In a moment of sudden awakening, a Buddhist meditation practitioner experiences going outside all *conditions*, which are merely phenomenal. The *Avatamsaka Sutra* presents a view of this limitless space of freedom in the best way of employing language.[23] Then the readers of the sutra are supposed to feel blissfully placed outside all phenomenal situations. Let us be careful about this point. I do not mean that all readers will have exactly the same experience, nor do I mean that those readers who go through that experience will be clearly aware that they are doing so. I propose instead that although readers will not be clearly aware of it, the text has the power

---

[23] Paul Demiéville, "The Mirror of the Mind," in *Sudden and Gradual Enlightenment: Approaches to Enlightenment in Chinese Thought*, ed. Peter N. Gregory (Honolulu: University of Hawai'i Press, 1987), 15.

to direct their attention out of the ego. The experiencer is "distinct from all conceptual orders."[24]

I would like to distinguish this feeling of bliss from the ordinary kind of happiness we usually experience in mundane life. We must keep a positive attitude toward the infinite whole. It is a spiritual feeling, which is the ground of all feelings. The blissfulness of this stillness is serene joy rather than the feeling of happiness. This is the feeling that lets you know the solid fact that the gates to Paradise are open right before you, or that there is no gate to the whole universe. I would like to point out that this joy is that to which Levinas, the great ethical philosopher, dedicates a large portion of *Totality and Infinity*, calling it "*jouissance*," translated as "enjoyment" in English.[25] Lacan, the psychoanalyst, also refers to it by this term.

Nevertheless, we also have to be keenly aware that pure enjoyment or bliss is *what the ego experiences*. According to Levinas, it is the state in which the ego expands and also contracts. To me, this sensibility of quiet bliss is very close to what contemporary spiritual teachers such as Eckhart Tolle, Mooji, Wilber, and Adyashanti, just to name a few, call "(pure) consciousness," "(pure) awareness," or "presence" (in a different sense from presence as opposed to absence). Those spiritual leaders are not traditional Western thinkers, nor are they academic thinkers such as Levinas, Lacan, and Deleuze who go against the traditional mode of Western metaphysics. I propose that now is the time that the leaders of the two fields—intellectuality (academia) and spirituality—have dialogues. *If they make an effort to communicate with each other and to be inspired by each other, they will certainly better serve humanity in general. Academic studies will have a clear goal to explore spirituality, and spiritual teachers will have better ways of clearly explaining enlightenment to help more audiences lead spiritual lives.*

Yet it seems that philosophers, spiritual teachers, authors, and artists just play separately and do not want to collaborate. I would like to suggest that they open their minds and try together for humanity itself. Buddhist (and Taoist) philosophy in general would be a bridge for them.

---

[24] Luis O. Gomez, "Purifying Gold: The Metaphor of Effort and Intuition in Buddhist Thought and Practice," in *Sudden and Gradual Enlightenment: Approaches to Enlightenment in Chinese Thought*, ed. Peter N. Gregory (Honolulu: University of Hawai'i Press, 1987), 85.

[25] See Emmanuel Levinas, *Totality and Infinity: An Essay on Exteriority*, trans. Alphonso Lingis (Pittsburgh: Duquesne University Press, 1992), in particular Section II.B, "Enjoyment and Representation," Section II.C, "I and Dependence," and Section III.A, "Sensibility and the Face."

On the one hand, contemporary philosophers of postmodern ethics are very close to Buddhist thought, whether they openly recognize it or not. After all is said and done, if the Western metaphysical tradition up until the emergence of postmodern ethics has not been following the whole, or the truth inside and outside, what has it been pursuing?

It is just that contemporary thinkers realize and point out that Western metaphysics has clung too intensely to reason and conceptualization. Kant, who clearly understood the indivisible and incomprehensible noumena over phenomena and became the pathfinder of modern Western philosophy, entitled his major books *Critique of Pure Reason, Critique of Practical Reason,* and *Critique of Judgment.* In America, Ralph Waldo Emerson (1803-1882) and Henry David Thoreau (1817-1862) employed the word "reason" to indicate a higher dimension than mere understanding.

On the other hand, almost all spiritual teachers make clear that their spiritual views and experiences are deeply based on Shakyamuni's teaching and Buddhism. There are special programs for mental and physical improvement such as "Mindfulness-Based Stress Reduction" (MBSR), developed by Jon Kabat-Zinn at the University of Massachusetts Medical Center since the 1970s. Those teachers and their programs rely mainly on the Theravada Buddhist style and the Zen style. It is my sincere desire that philosophers, all in the humanities field, spiritual leaders, literary authors and artists in general, academic thinkers, and spiritual leaders try to be more open to each other. If scholars provide secular and religious leaders with an academic grounding, the two groups will together advance the human mind. We can then take advantage of the studies of literature, film, and other arts for the same goal. A critic's role is important for the public's understanding.

Literature and film make us feel cheerful and laugh and allow us to experience sorrowful and painful situations. Reading a story or viewing images on a screen with sounds places us in certain moods of the situations that we can possibly experience in our own daily lives. While literature allows us to have more freedom of imagination, films require us to follow affective events and characters who lead our imagination. Films provide us with a great deal of information in a very short period of time. Yet film has the power to affect us with concrete examples from real-life stories. It can engage us more closely and effectively in the narrative with various techniques involving images and sound. The common goal for both literature and film is to lead the audience outside any possible theme and imagination—mainly by showing the tragic conclusion of the dream of the main character. Two main categories of film-producing techniques are montage and mise-en-scène. Montage is the work of editing film by cutting it up that involves many other smaller techniques and modifying time sequences according to the narrative that will be projected on the screen. In contrast, mise-en-scène is the process by which all of the actors, cameras, and other things are put together on the spot for one scene. Sometimes it takes a lot of work to produce excellent effects.

Flashback and close-up are two of the main techniques for blurring the concepts of time sequencing. *Citizen Kane* (starring and directed and produced by Orson Welles, 1941), the great Hollywood classic, is well-known for the great effect of its use of the flashback technique. This technique shows Kane's younger days and older years. "Deep-focus" is another cinematographic technique that is used to simultaneously show clear visions of the middle ground, the background, as well as the foreground. Kane's innocence is revealed in the opening scene, which is shown later again as a flashback, in which he drops a snow globe saying "Rosebud." Rosebud is the name of the snow sleigh he used to play with in his childhood, and it reveals his pure heart to us. Even though he is a man of extreme wealth and fame, Kane has secretly adhered to his purity, and the story discloses his stubbornness to us. He is just a "citizen," a normal person, not a man who is special.

There is no doubt that those whom Wolfgang Iser (1926-2007), a prominent German reader-response critic, named "implied" readers and other reader-response critics call "real" readers would accept the most sensitive spiritual sublimity. However, it is critical that the implied or real readers are not those who are simply ready to accept the given ideas or a theme that totalizes the text. I demonstrate in the following chapters how the implied or real readers would respond more sensitively when they are engaged with the given narrative. I agree with Iser that the literary text is not just an object to be thematically interpreted by readers in any way. The given literary or cinematic narrative lays bare the reality of the egoic dream. Through the details of characters and settings, readers are led to the Middle Way, beyond the polarities of binary opposites and multiplication. The clear distinction between good and evil, right and wrong, and superiority and inferiority becomes blurred. Through their wandering viewpoints, readers are expected to be guided to encounter the ultimate reality of life.

The ultimate reality is the dimension of non-duality, where every being and every thing is not one, but not two. All forms are different, yet all forms are interconnected to all others in one network. All different forms come into being in terms of codependent arising, and they are in oneness, like all the jewels that constitute Indra's net in *Avatamsak Sutra*. In other words, the relationships are the appearance of the subjects-objects, yet in the ultimate reality, they are truly one. The seer is the seen. Going one step further, the essence of all deserves the names "absolute truth," "infinity," or God.

Those phenomena of cherished dreams reveal to us, the audience, that the protagonists' innocence, the fundamental human desire, is pursued in the form of pure love. Another example of such a story is *The Great Gatsby* (published in 1925 and released as a film in 1974 and 2013). In *The Great Gatsby*, what is "great" is the pure love of Gatsby's innocent, uncontaminated mind for a woman. He has that pure love even though he knows that she is now married to another man.

From our spiritual perspective, those phenomenal desires are merely different forms of the genuine desire for the ultimate reality. The ultimate reality is beyond literary texts or films, which are only phenomenal for us to perceive and empirically understand. Although it is also what creates the phenomena of the story, scenes, sound, and other techniques, the ultimate reality in itself is informationless. Yet we can only go through the experience of glimpsing it, and going through great examples of it would be experiencing the aesthetic sublime.

Another word for the ultimate reality is Emptiness, and it is the same as *dharmakaya*, or the Buddha body, which transcends the phenomena of five senses. It is a detrimental misunderstanding to think that it nihilistically means the absence of power or the energy of presence. It is a nihilist's misunderstanding with a folly that is caused by their pessimistic habit that Emptiness is an inanimate zone. In contrast, it means infinite freedom and activity; it both embraces and does not attach to either presence or absence. Emptiness is the most profound dimension where all phenomena arise in terms of *dependent co-origination,* without any inherent privilege given to anyone or anyone.[26]

As the supreme example of a *kongan,* Seon Buddhists usually take the flower sermon of Shakyamuni Buddha as the first case of the transmission of his spiritual teaching. The story of the flower sermon relates that when the Buddha, without a word, picked up a flower and showed it to a great many disciples and followers, only Mahakasyapa, who later became the successor (the second patriarch) of Shakyamuni, understood what he meant by so doing, and smiled at the Buddha. Then the Buddha conferred dharma, the whole body of teachings he expounded, on him and sanctioned him as the second patriarch.[27]

In this story, the transmission of supreme spirituality is done wordlessly, which means that the spiritual dimension is pre-linguistic and preconceptual, and thus cannot be explained in language, which is constituted with

---

[26] Humphries, *Reading Emptiness*, 32.
[27] William Harmless, S. J., *Mystics* (Oxford: Oxford University Press, 2008), 192.

conceptualization. Conceptualization is composed plainly of polar opposites—right cannot be identified without wrong, and good is good because there is the concept of bad or evil. *Kongans* and *hwadus* are the devices to follow this method of spiritual transmission that takes place in the Transmiddle Zone, which does not appear as either of the two opposites. The Transmiddle Path, the value-free middle way, is always a matter of paramount importance, but it also eludes the empirical zone. The Seon tradition—from its first patriarch, Master Bodhidharma, who had come from India—had the unchanging principle that language is unable to carry transcendental spirituality.

The anecdote of Buddha showing the flower to his disciples and Mahakasyapa's spiritual comprehension or acceptance are the forms that carry spirituality, which is not a perceivable message. It is remarkable that in the Seon Buddhist tradition, spiritual significance transcends any possible theme of *kongans* or any sutras, and thus language cannot straightforwardly reach the dharma. The ineffable nature of the spiritual dharma, transmitted from the Buddha to Mahakasyapa, is not based on any theory or abstraction. What this wordless sermon, as the first *kongan*, presents to us is the exterior of any given phenomenal story or situation.

In this way, *kongans* and *hwadus* do not show us any subject or message that is to be intellectually understood. They aim for a spiritual transmission that is possible outside the teaching of the scriptures. What is the spirituality that should be taught wordlessly from one person to another? Although it takes a form that is exactly the specific situation that takes place in its context, genuine spirituality is what is termed *Sunyata*, or "Emptiness." That is to say, *kongans* and *hwadus* aim to lead us beyond the limits of conceptualization—the dimension empty of the flow of time and space that we firmly seize as the grounds of our existence.

Each moment of life as "what appears there" is connected to "what does not appear there." Not simply nihilistic nothingness or a void, Emptiness is *perfect emptiness with wondrous movement*. As movement, Emptiness embraces both presence and absence and refuses to be attached to either; it transcends both, and it also is immanent in both. It is the actual ground, or true nature, of what is changing and transitory. Every phenomenon arises in Emptiness, and it finally returns to Emptiness. It means that the dual structure of a phenomenon comes to be deconstructed and returns to Emptiness. This process can be called "self-deconstruction." Speaking in a more accurate way, every instant of a phenomenon is a different appearance of Emptiness.

Let me continue exploring this self-deconstructive nature of humans in more detail. Humans wish to achieve success and pursue happiness, and they usually think of happiness at a superficial level. Yet spirituality at the core of humanity that lies beyond the ontological nature of appearance and personality is *not* egoistic and does not separate itself from others. If you seriously look into the depth of humanity and the world, you would find that, at a fundamental level, all human activities, in reality, carry self-deconstruction—not only literature and the arts but also other areas.

We human beings think and act, even to the extent of fighting and killing in war, in order to live in peace and love. We are fundamentally spiritual, but our phenomenal appearances are always identified as either good or bad in a given situation. The duality takes all of our minds, as we do not know or are not interested in spirituality. Although we do not properly understand our inner nature, the ultimate reality is truly different. We all actually wish to attain true happiness, not the mere pleasure that we feel with our five senses. In deep reality, we want *spiritual* happiness, despite the fact that they usually do not realize it. For example, when politicians or business people do their jobs, many of them may take it for granted that they just want more political power or money. They would not truly concern themselves with others' well-being. Yet, deep inside their mind, or below their consciously knowing mind, humans are pursuing genuine happiness for all. That is the real purpose of humanity and society. They are just unaware of their true purpose and fight with each other.

Living a self-deconstructive spiritual life without attachment to phenomenal objects (ourselves included), as the *Tao-te Ching* says, we would live in the way that doing is not doing, moving is unmoving, speaking is not speaking, individually thinking in the limitless whole. Of all fields of human life and the world, literature and the arts are distinctive in that they are more intensely minded to have the goal of reaching outside the ego. More specifically, while the main purpose of fine arts and music is to arouse our emotions so that our imaginative capacity is incited, literature as the art of language makes us draw on logical reasoning as well as feelings to activate our imagination.

Indeed, literature is "a privileged ground for the realization of emptiness," that is, for breaking the fundamental illusion that the finite ego construct generates.[28] Film as a synthetic art form is certainly characteristic of this nature. The exterior of what we experience as objective reality is the infinite. Literature works just like a *kongan,* an anecdote that bears an unreasonable solution to problems in the given situation. Again, the characteristic of literature and the arts is that they "pave ways for the self of the reader to escape the binary opposition and have a universal consciousness."[29]

---

[28] Humphries, *Reading Emptiness*, 45.
[29] Lee, *Postmodern Ethics*, 10.

However, the usual style of reading to find a theme or main message cannot serve our purpose. In most cases of reading literary works—whether a short or a long novel, a drama, or a poem—readers are trying to find a theme that the text seems to build. They end up discussing and judging whether the theme is good or bad on the basis of morality or according to the ethics of the specific period and culture in which the text was written. Speaking from this very limited perspective, every element of a literary story is perceivable, and nothing lies outside what is written. The goal of the author's writing is to claim the main message and support it with imaginary circumstances, and the goal of the reader is to find the theme set by the author.

In this classic view, a literary work is a very good example of the cultural artifact that reflects the totality of the society and the age. Although it is one aspect of literature and film, we should not restrict art within these narrow limits. First and foremost, literature and film are works of art! Are they not so? Literature, if you will, is so in the sense that it can go deep into our mind and arouse our imagination without establishing ready-made scenes that limit our imagination. I am convinced that no one would disagree on this. A literary text does not philosophize a topic as a philosophical book does, nor does it only report news. In either case, we readers are supposed to understand literally what the text says. If we read a literary text in this way, the goal of reading would be no different from that of reading a philosophical text or a newspaper article. In a more plain way, the aim of a literary text would be the same as the advertisement of a product. The text is the author's device to let the reader understand and accept their idea, just as the advertisement of a product is to persuade those who see it to buy the product.

Well, in the history of aesthetics and literary criticism, such a stereotypical view largely lasted until the end of modernism. In modernism proper, such a seemingly right theme as the totality of the text was considered of utmost importance. Yet this view had already failed even before the end of modernism. Many late modernist authors such as Virginia Woolf, T. S. Eliot, and James Joyce, just to name a few, were far from this traditional style of writing, although they had nostalgia for modernism.

In the new era of postmodernism, modernism is now much more harshly criticized for its tyranny of the Enlightenment (in the Western sense), which necessarily needed rigid rules for governing a nation, and for a totalizing theme in literary criticism. In the new era of postmodernity, that is, the age of postmodernism *per se,* and especially *postmodern ethics,* what is critical is not the subject or message but how the literary text leads us to realize what lies deep down in our mind, what we are in our *transphenomenal* state or outside of language itself. That the ultimate reality, or Emptiness with wondrous movement in the Buddhist sense, and the text is, just like one's life, a *form* that Emptiness takes in a given culture and era.

Although the public has the false expectation of enjoying a story with a happy ending, actual masterpieces do not offer the audience a superficially happy ending. Masterpieces rather present stories of the protagonist suffering and usually end with a tragic conclusion. Real happiness is not the shallow feeling of pleasure, and thus a happy ending does not make us experience true happiness. Literature leads us to the ineffable ultimate reality of human life, and that is why it shows the destruction of the form of life. In the light of postmodern ethics, a literary work or film has an intensely inherent *irony*. The irony is never some character unique to the literature and film. The form of our mind, our society, our world, and everything we do is in the form of binary opposition, which continuously produces ironies. A literary story consists of a continuum of struggles between polar opposites all the way to the end, and at the end these struggles do not meet with proper solutions.

Rather, a literary text that seriously deals with life's problems shows a continuous eruption of conflicts and ongoing battles between the opposing sides up to the end of the story. A masterpiece, which strikes an enduring chord in the public mind, does not offer us the mere sensation of satisfaction and superficial happiness. Art has the power to enable us to confront the source of true happiness. We would see that the dualism of a literary story *deconstructs* the story itself. Not only the conclusion but the story as a whole aim to awaken the reader from the delusion of the ego. We do not have to do anything crucial because self-deconstruction is the essential nature of art, and we just have to unveil the depth of the literary work. A story as a dualistic (egoistic) construct naturally self-deconstructs.

The protagonist undergoes a downfall and, in many cases, dies. Through a tragic novel or drama in which the main character suffers extreme sorrow and pain, we experience the sublime feelings that lead us beyond ordinary sensations. We come to experience sublime feelings, especially from a consequence of the protagonist's tragic flaw, moral weakness, or inability to cope with unpropitious conditions that often bring very sad events involving the protagonist's death. A masterpiece consists of a continuum of the hero or heroine's struggle between polar opposites all the way to the end. It actually deconstructs the dual form of any possible theme, and the reader's intellect and sense turn outside the dual form of mind. In this sense, literature, film, and other arts empower our minds to see the aesthetic nature of self-deconstruction, which also happens in Ch'an/Seon/Zen Buddhist meditation to attain enlightenment. The power of religion and art leads us to the solid truth of non-ego or no-self. Only the non-ego is the true self.

Therefore, the reader, just like the Buddhist meditation practitioner, goes through the tough work of reaching the ultimate reality. The irrational story, which is not as expected by the reader, is just like a *kongan* story. The import of the *hwadu* (keyword) from the Buddhist meditation "What is it?" works appropriately in literary reading. Such an important question leads the reader through various events that show the impermanence of phenomena of life in the given story. The story as a whole is just like the process of "doubting" the false truths of phenomenal elements of all other existences than the unconditioned, and thus limitless, true self of the reader. "What is it?" shares the same goal with the tragic end of a literary text—to lead one outside the ego circuit.

The ultimate reality is Emptiness, precisely as the *Avatamsaka Sutra* tells us, which embodies the grandeur of the universe to which Shakyamuni Buddha awakened. While phenomena in the world and universe seem conflicting to us, the essence of the entire universe is perfectly unobstructed and seamless. The *Avatamsaka Sutra* has been interpreted in English as the *Flower Garland Sutra, Flower Adornment Sutra,* or *Hua-yen Sutra.* Though not widely known in the West, it is one of the most important sutras in Mahayana Buddhism. The translator of a complete version of this sutra in a thick volume, Thomas Cleary, affirms that the *Avatamsaka Sutra* is "what many have considered the most grandiose, the most comprehensive, and the most beautifully arrayed of the Buddhist scriptures."[30]

This sutra portrays the ultimate reality, or the true nature of all of us, phenomenally in language for ordinary Buddhists and the public. Hua-yen is the magnificent scenery of the cosmos decorated with an unlimited amount of flowers. By reading a superb sutra such as the *Avatamsaka Sutra,* we can experience liberation from the conditional ego, going through a stage that is similar to the *Samadhi,* the more intense version of the aesthetic sublime. We would realize that, as the *Avatamsaka Sutra* says, in the ultimate reality, we are all *no less than Vairocana,* the celestial primordial Buddha. "Detachment from the World," Book 38 of the *Avatamsaka Sutra,* says that we have the spiritual power "to comprehend the inherent essence of all things."[31] Beyond question, "the inherent essence of all things" is the Buddha-nature, and "all things are like phantoms" and "illusions." The Buddha-nature as the essence is Christ's consciousness in Christian terms

---

[30] Thomas Cleary, *Entry Into the Inconceivable: An Introduction to Hua-Yen Buddhism* (Honolulu: University of Hawai'i Press, 1983).

[31] Thomas Cleary, trans., *The Flower Ornament Scripture: A Translation of the Avatamsaka Sutra* (Boston: Shambhala Publications, Inc., 1993), 1032.

or *the dancing light* as in the title of this book. The non-dual light of truth always freely engenders dual-natured phenomena.

3.4. Literature and Buddhists' sudden awakening

I would like to explain how literary reading is exactly related to Buddhism in greater detail. I have said above that the sublime offers the reader the effect of glimpsing enlightenment. However, I do not mean that the aesthetic effect of the sublime is as strong as the moment of sudden enlightenment. A genuine moment of enlightenment as explained in Buddhism would surely be much more intense and powerful than the moment of the sublime that a literary reader or a film viewer experiences. However, it is clear that the real goal of the sublime is to lead the reader or viewer beyond language itself and have an opportunity to encounter the ultimate reality. This experience has the same nature as meditation and other practices in Buddhism. As the given story reaches a climax and conclusion, the reader comes to be placed outside all the situations described in the literary work of art. In both cases of experiencing the exterior, the experiencer is "totally distinct from all conceptual orders."[32]

Both the meditation practitioner and the literary reader pass through the door to the dimension of spirituality, which the intellectual mind and language cannot reach. In Mahayana Buddhism, the *Avatamsaka Sutra* is considered to be the most representative one for instant enlightenment. It is commonly believed in Mahayana Buddhism that Shakyamuni expounded his experience of awakening in the *Avatamsaka Sutra* right after his sudden awakening that happened under the Bodhi tree. The *Lotus Sutra* and the *Nirvana Sutra* are also regarded as significant sutras that have the import of sudden enlightenment.[33] Enlightenment can come slowly, but it is commonly acknowledged that when a person has a breakthrough experience from the ordinary mind to the spiritual dimension, they experience it out of the blue!

However, it seems to me that *ghanhwa-seon* leaders have some problems. I propose that *ghanhwa-seon* leaders must adjust their way of thinking and meditation style to modern society's needs. For my part, I believe *ghanhwa-seon* is not a greatly recommendable style of meditation for beginners for the following reasons.

---

[32] Gomez, "Purifying Gold," 85.

[33] See Neal Donner, "Sudden and Gradual Intimately Conjoined: Chih-i's T'ien-t'ai View," in *Sudden and Gradual Enlightenment: Approaches to Enlightenment in Chinese Thought*, ed. Peter N. Gregory (Honolulu: University of Hawai'i Press, 1987), 201-226.

First, meditating on *hwadus* needs concentration that is only really possible for monks living in remote places deep in the mountains. Second, it is very difficult for the public, who live busy workaday lives in this day and age. For them, it would not be easy to concentrate on repeating the wording and meaning of it. The practitioner would easily be caught in mere repetitions of the wording of a *hwadu,* not relying upon the ultimate reality of the self, world, and universe.

Third, the traditional style masters of *ghanhwa-seon* are not kind, perhaps even rude, when leading the practitioners. Some of them still keep assuming the same attitude as harsh ancient masters did when teaching monks of their times. Some are still strongly inclined just to accuse the practitioner of a lack of ardor in being entirely immersed in the *hwadu* and staying in a state of doubt (concentration on questioning) about *Samadhi*. It is clear to me that such masters and teachers imitate those who taught their students more than a thousand years ago and are obviously unable to help Westerners understand and accept *ghanhwa-seon* with ease.

Fourth, as a result, the effect of that mundane kind of practice is not strong enough to make the practitioners remain in a stable state of mind in everyday life. I sincerely hope that they will remind themselves often that an efficient *gradual* process will result in a "sudden" awakening. For the modern public, the graduality of the process will have to be emphasized. Directing lay people and even monks in the way of obtaining a right and wise comprehension of the true self and world with reason and logic would produce a better result. In addition, the sudden awakening theory alone might bring a sense of mysticism.

Fifth, *ghanhwa-seon* masters must always remember that the technique of concentrating on and repeating crucial questions and positive words are already known in the West by those who practice different kinds of meditations such as silent illumination in the Zen tradition, Vipassana, and Tibetan meditation.

The globalization of *ghanhwa-seon* would not really be possible, therefore, unless the masters and teachers take kinder, applicable, and amiable attitudes to those of every walk of life who are eager to learn more about Buddhism and practice meditation. They also have to keep such an attitude for the scholars who want to seriously study it for academic purposes. Those strict and stubborn masters and teachers who confuse and frustrate those who are interested in *ghanhwa-seon* meditation would seem to the public to be rigid and self-centered. Such ancient style leaders, who maintain their idea that *ghanhwa-seon* is the unique way of abolishing the ego, must realize that they will have to be satisfied with having a little group of maniacs.

In fact, those strict masters of today misunderstand that those of the past were full of true love for their students and the public. It misunderstands well-known ancient masters' seeming strictness. The leaders of *ghanhwa-seon* meditation or any other type of meditation can succeed in helping others to attain their awakening and in making efforts to establish a more peaceful society—but only when they are exemplars of egoless and loving kind humans.

3.5. God as your true self in Christianity

I would like to devote the last part of this chapter to the conservative believers in Christianity and other major religions for the sake of their understanding of our issues regarding literature and film. I would first like to emphasize that the true God in Christianity is not different from Emptiness, or the ultimate truth, which is the final goal of literature and film. God is not egoistic but love itself, as the New Testament says (1 John 4:8). Other major religions share the same view of the love of God. Yes, many of you would agree that it is also commonsensical. The basic doctrinal issues of all of Christianity, Hinduism, Islam, and Buddhism claim that God loves people. However, it is also accurate to say that religions stick to their own doctrinal dogmas regarding what kind of followers can be loved by God. Above all, it is for certain that fundamental theologians and believers simply hold on to the view that God loves the believers of His own religion.

With respect to that fact, Buddhism has more merits than others. Buddhism in general, and the Mahayana tradition in particular, does not adhere to such a narrow view. In Mahayana Buddhism, the Buddha is never an egoistic figure who loves his own people. From my unbiased perspective, it is crystal clear that in the heart of Christianity, God is the great Creator of the universe, and yet in my sense, this means that God is the unnameable substance of both the presence and absence of all phenomena. God, as the most embracing substance, continues to create through the life of every one of us. God constantly creates new situations and a new world through us. God creates in the past, the present, and the future, and we are part of his creation (2 Cor. 5:17; Gal. 6:15). He creates the presence of being and phenomena from nothing, non-phenomenality. As we sense the exteriority of time and space, we come to be truly new spiritual beings.

Why? In Christian terms, it is because he wants to affirm his loftiness and enjoy it. But in the context of our discussion and communication, God is the pure consciousness/awareness of ourselves. Yet God's enjoyment is surely of the nature of deepest love—which has been called "*agape*"—or even beyond it, not love as a feeling of being attached to the object. In the innermost part of our being, we are "pure consciousness/awareness," and it is the whole; that is, we are God on the most fundamental level, and it also means that we are all *one*. The rest of the binary structure is characteristic of the egoic attachment, which is expressed symbolically in the Bible to have started with the eating of the fruit.

You can comprehend the heart of Buddhism that I explain in this book only if you have the desire to allow yourself to consider that the Buddha or Buddha-nature is fundamentally the same as God or the Kingdom of Heaven.

To speak in terms of secular spirituality, as Ramana Maharshi, one of the most respected spiritual leaders in the West, says, *God is within you as you*. God is your genuine, infinite self. This is "your" true self, but also the collective human self or that of the universe. God is (pure) consciousness—consciousness that always wants to affirm His own nature by seeing His images reflected in us, the world, and the universe. He is the ultimate, universal consciousness that is everyone's real I, not the perceivable I, which lies beyond time and space. God is out of the reach of our intellectual knowing and the capability to use language. God wants to *enjoy* His creation.

In line with Deleuze and Levinas, you can say that God's endless creation is carried out at the point which is closest to our presence in terms of "pure becoming" and purely "ethical" human relations. In this sense, we can also say that God is a movement that establishes all relations (behind them) in which we affect each other, especially ethical relations. The Spirit is like the power that is beyond, and also in the heart of, Yin and Yang. Yin and Yang are opposites in one, and God's Holy Spirit moves the opposites for constant creation.

In this way, God in us is always creating, and we must surrender to God. The nature of ultimate reality does not belong to any stability. God is Emptiness with wondrous movement. God not only continues creation through us but destroys. God is beyond the phenomena but is also within the phenomena. The movement of the Truth is not phenomenal, but it is the source of the phenomena. We are expected to dance to the flow of the Spirit of the Truth. This means that we follow the most natural cause-and-effect movements, whether within our relations with others or within the relations of the two different sides of our individual mind. We should follow the natural flow of what is inside us, not attaching our mind to the outward values of phenomena.

Buddhism describes this in much clearer ways. The *Heart Sutra,* one of the primary texts in Mahayana Buddhism, says: "Emptiness is form, form is emptiness." The appearance and state of every being, every thing, and every phenomenon are just the outward forms that Emptiness or God takes. It is because everything, even Dharma, another name for the Truth, is a movement, and nothing is in a stable, fixed state. Buddha told his disciples that even though he had taught for 50 years, he really taught nothing. He meant that all of his teachings were for people to comprehend and sense the non-duality of ultimate truth, which does not need any phenomenal expression that is in the form of binary opposition.

In Catholicism, centering/contemplative prayer or Jesus prayer mainly takes the meditative form. There has been a tradition of silent prayer in Catholicism, especially in the Eastern Orthodox Church, and even in Protestantism. St. Francis of Assisi (1181/1182-1226) and St. Teresa of Ávila (1515-1582) were prominent mystic, Roman Catholic saints who led contemplative lives through mental prayer. In the 20th century, Fr. Thomas Merton (1915-1968) was well-known for contemplative prayer, and in the present, Fr. Thomas Keating (1923-) and Fr. Richard Rohr (1943-) are representative leaders of centering prayer. Centering/contemplative prayer leads believers to the middle of stillness. (Stillness in this sense is in the middle of turbulent situations or even in war, as well as the phenomenal silence coming from outside.) The phrases often employed by those who pray are "God, have mercy on me," "Be still and know that I am God," or "Jesus" or "love" in short forms. These phrases work like *hwadus* in the keyword meditation of Ch'an/Seon/Zen Buddhism.

In this light, literature and film guide us to this ultimate source of true happiness, peace, and joy beyond all situations of conflicts in life. Literary reading and meditation let us go deep into the ultimate reality, which is already a movement. The ultimate reality is none other than our true self!

CHAPTER FOUR

MEDITATION THROUGH TWO MASTERPIECES: *HAMLET* AND *MOBY-DICK* AS VAST *KONGANS*

4.1. How are literature and film meant to help free you from your ego intensity?

To continue with religion, Christianity, Buddhism, and other religions surely teach us to use the fundamentally dual nature of the mind as a tool to embody and concretize the truth to make the world better. To elaborate on this point, it is clear to me that the Christian Bible, Buddhist sutras, and the scriptures of other religions should not be taken literally. They must be read as different descriptions of the source of the ultimate reality of humanity that lies beyond the finitude of the ego. The ultimate reality is not limited to any one religion. However, fundamentalism is made up of egoic ideas. Fundamentalism has merits to planting faith in one's mind and strengthening it. But more than that, fundamentalism refuses to listen to the deep levels of mythic, metaphorical, and mystical meaning, and unquestionably the ineffable truth that lies beyond. It is obsessed with literalism and exclusion. The egoic need for clarity and certitude leads fundamentalists to use sacred writings in a mechanical, closed-ended, and quite authoritarian manner. The ego rarely asks real questions about life and the true self. Most of the time, when it comes to the real question, the ego gives quick and easy answers that you (the ego itself) would favor. This invariably leads the ego-driven mind to build groups and societies. Humans have been utterly trapped in these self-built conditions throughout history. Thus they miss liberating messages along with the deepest challenges and consolations of the Gospels and Buddhist scriptures.

Hence, having spiritual power has to be seen in our everyday mundane lives—doing whatever we do in general, reading literary texts, watching films, and appreciating other arts. That is, finding truth does not mean you lose interest in the practicality of living in society and secluding yourself from society by living in a remote place. Unless you really desire to live as a monk or nun, you can and should try to reach the spiritual goal in your life. As you grow spiritually, you would live in a much more lively way with more energy, not being so attached to trivial things. You would pursue what seems to lie beyond immediate pleasures and short-term goals. Instead of enjoying competition with others for inconsequential objects, you would have a stronger interest in the ways of exploring spirituality and infinity in the reality of daily life. You would simply do whatever you do while you appreciate and dwell in not knowing, which renowned Korean Seon master Seungsahn (1927-2004) called "don't-know mind."

The first source of the study of the ego should be the fields of religion and philosophy, and psychoanalysis is an extremely significant foundation for thoughts on the growth of the ego as consciousness. In academia, Sigmund Freud, the founder of psychoanalysis, thought the ego was the real power for life, but Jacques Lacan, who interpreted Freud's theory in his linguistic and poststructural view, contrariwise considered the ego as an illusion. The ego is by nature the selfish power that falls short of the true reality. "The mirror stage" Lacan describes as the formation of the ego through the self-objectifying process is a process by which one is alienated from "the Real," one's true, unutterable self. Lacan's harsh objection against American ego psychology, whose purpose is to enhance the ego power to have a healthy mental power, is well-known.[34] Of course, it is necessary for an infant to start to have a structure of the ego as their mental function and that a child goes through healthy stages of ego development. We cannot demand that a child gets rid of the ego before their wholesome development. However, in the long run, from the perspective of spirituality beyond mental function, the ego is not conscious. Especially from the perspective of spirituality, it is, on the contrary, unconscious of what is truly going on in the ultimate reality.

Nevertheless, it is time to pay more attention to the arts, especially literature and film. It is perfectly clear to me that, just like Buddhist philosophy, literary reading has the aim of removing the practitioner's ego power of attachment to untrue and unreliable pleasure through its story and mood, and thus to make the ego frame merely a tool of the real self. As I explain throughout this work, reading literature as a form of meditation would certainly be a very effective way to abolish the ego construct and confront the momentum of enlightenment in the very situation of our mundane workaday life. Nowhere else would actually be the very place for you to encounter a sudden spiritual awakening and cultivate your spirituality.

---

[34] For Lacan, there are three psychological orders—the Real, the Imaginary, and the Symbolic. The Imaginary forms the primary illusion, which means the birth of narcissism, and the Symbolic is the order of producing language.

At the same time, what should be acknowledged is that we do not practice meditation simply to reduce stress and feel "happy" or satisfied without disturbance. A retreat into seclusion is for intense practice, not simply to escape social relations. Staying in a meditative state in daily life would determine the pattern of the repetitive return of the ego and expose the *dancing, creating* light of universal intelligence, and thus true freedom. Because the light moves ceaselessly, engendering all, it is right to say that it expresses itself. The light of real liberty and the knowledge of infinity take the form of wisdom as it appears in the frame of a story you read and the mood you feel, and eventually in the sublime you experience.

To overcome the problem of the ego as the root of self-conflict should not be understood as anything different from the best way of understanding the literary work or film's purpose. As readers and viewers, we are expected to experience the destruction of the structure of the binary opposition, where the power of attachment arises. The literary story or film shows how the protagonist's egoic life collapses due to its binary or dual nature. In light of the theoretical view we discussed in the previous three chapters, the polar opposites cause self-conflict due to their self-contradictoriness.

Taking sides is attaching to one of the opposites and being stuck to it, as the ego judges it to be the truth. However, either one always has its opposite. It is phenomenally so, unmistakably, because the ego's thinking goes that way. All is due to the phenomenal split in the ego. Because of this split, when the ego confronts any being (including itself) or social situation as an object, it sees the object also in a split form. In other words, as the seer has a double structure, so does the seen.

The true self is behind or beyond the double caused by the split inside the ego. Once gone beyond the finite double, it is undoubtedly universal and even beyond, since each and every thing and being is a phenomenon comprised by the double. The double is the very primal force that gives birth to a phenomenon, and this means that the ego is split. It is the false self, and the true self as the whole as such is never seen as phenomenal.

Despite how long it lives, the finite ego is very limited. The ego has to realize the nuclear truth that it is an illusion of unlimitedness, that it is already "enlightened" or awakened to its own universalness. In the ultimate fact, nature even transcends the universal nature. Yet beyond, beneath, or behind the ego's discerning thinking, the whole lies as the truth of the phenomenon of the double.

Although it can be said that an individual life, society, world, and history follow the ultimate reality, the special devices to fulfill this purpose are literature, film, and other mediums—paintings, fine arts, music, etc. For our main discussion, literature as the art of language appeals both to our reason and to our emotion. I propose that literary stories bring both a conceptual mind and the emotions of the reader not to an ideology but to the Transmiddle Path, where everything is deconstructed and Emptiness is looming. The end of a literary text as an artwork rather blurs the distinction between good and bad, beautiful and ugly, and identifies it and eliminates it. After reading the whole text, you are left alone without more of the story. The reader is left in the preconceptual dimension.

Due to the fact that the story is not your own life story and thus cannot strike you, it can leave only you with apathy. You might not have any feeling, or you might have the feeling of the void. Yet the feeling of apathy is the core of the aesthetic sublime, as Nancy explains. It means that, whether you feel like taking any meditative posture or form, you are ready for meditation. You may want to simply think more and feel as if you are still in the mood of the literary writing or the movie, especially thanks to the sublime feeling you experienced. Because the sublime feeling is a mixture of pleasure and pain, you might think you are confused. This is OK. There is nothing wrong with your feeling so. It is the moment of gazing into the dimension of the real self as Emptiness. Otherwise, it might be a stifled feeling, or a sad and tragic feeling, not happiness and satisfaction. (In fact, serious literary works for an adult audience would not offer you a happy ending.) The feeling would not be strong because the reader is not the one who has experienced the story first-hand. It is someone else's story. In any case, you, the reader or viewer, are guided to the Emptiness, or at least to ambiguous sensibility.

Yet the specific sense you feel would have a lasting impact with regard to the fundamentality of being alive. The artwork raises a question that is not known to your intellect, and that it is why masterpieces have left the strong and lasting effect of keeping us in the empty center of life. The Emptiness of the center of life means everything, and all phenomena, including ourselves, are empty—wholly empty, without phenomenal identity. Again, however, it must be remembered that Emptiness is the power of the wondrous movement that yields the sequences of time and space. The masterpieces do not set any theme as a main message that totalizes the whole work in a concrete form. They show our ego is deconstructed and led to the empty core, or how our life as a whole is actually completely empty and yet also a priceless dance-like movement.

The sublime feeling can take the form of deep, genuine happiness or the bliss of experiencing the fountain of life itself in the middle of tragic situations, pain, or serious illness. In the Christian Bible, a supreme example would be Job's story in the Book of Job, part of the Old Testament. In daily life, such cases occasionally happen to people who are going through exceptional situations. Nevertheless, there are many well-known religious figures whose lives were completely changed after experiencing a spiritual breakthrough. More than that, today, we actually see many secular spiritual teachers who have experienced the swift spiritual transformation from the egoic state to the preconceptual dimension after the transformation. To the ego, the dimension of preconceptuality is the blind spot, the unperceivable, the space between happy feelings and feelings of pain. The Buddhist term for this zone is the "Middle Path," but, as I have explained since the beginning of this book, for the sake of the general reader's understanding, I describe it as the "Transmiddle" path because the "middle" does not indicate the phenomenal zone between the opposites that comprise the binary opposition of the ego's decision, but rather the whole of the two.

I would like to claim that true happiness is what you feel while on the way to the Transmiddle Path—genuine Emptiness—and that deep, true happiness is prior to the experience of ordinary happy feelings or pleasure. Then the Transmiddle Path is the most fundamental ground of the whole universe, where every thing and every being arises and disappears according to the cause and effect that takes place.

As the most concretely described literary work for our discussion of the sublime feeling (both aesthetic and spiritual), which brings us to face the true self, I always refer to Robert Louis Stevenson's *The Strange Case of Dr. Jekyll and Mr. Hyde* (1886). When it comes to the matter of the (ethical) self-deconstruction of the literary work, this story strikes me first because it is the most concrete example. I will elaborate on this novella in detail in the next chapter. Just to mention it as an example here, the socially respected, decent-looking Jekyll and the hideous-looking, murderous Hyde comprise the personality of one person. Jekyll is overwhelmed with the exclusive sense of being a decent doctor with a respectable personality, and he denies the essential half that comprises the whole of his existence together with that egoistic self. Jekyll's egoic sense of "me"-centered certainty results in his wish to cut off the evil nature from his social identity as a respected doctor by committing suicide. The truth Jekyll does not know is that he has to embrace Hyde in any way because he cannot exist without the wild and violent nature of Hyde. In order to embrace the other side of his own personality, Jekyll must detach himself from his social identity as a respected doctor and face Hyde with equanimity.

Jekyll's story reflects why we need to detach ourselves from a state of agitation, anger, pride, jealousy, avarice, greed, hate, and even love and happiness as feelings of attachment. In other words, one should let go of their tenacity of being attached to one idea (usually one's own idea) regarding a situation. We should acknowledge the middle ground where various possibilities—either clear or unclear and dim—are laid. The middle ground may mean no idea to many, yet it is actually like an ocean of possibilities. Metaphorically speaking, life, which is transitory in any case, is a ripple that arises from the ocean. However surging and turbulent the ripple is, it soon subsides. In fact, all different kinds of events in life that constitute what we call "reality" consist of tiny movements like ripples. The ego twists the vision of the ocean and makes the ripple consider itself only as a severed, tiny entity. Any image or idea that separates you as superior to the limitless is an ego-made idol, ego ideal, or ideal ego in psychoanalytic terms. That image always results in comparing and contrasting yourself and others, and then superiority or inferiority to others. Superiority brings self-conceit, inferiority, stress, and pain.

As you read literary texts in the ways I elaborate here in the present work, you can realize the real purpose of the text as an artwork—especially from the spiritual perspective. The purpose of literary reading (and eventually reading the world) is that we have opportunities to lose the insatiable avidity of the ego and enter the space of the real self—the realm of real, deeper, or mature happiness and genuine wisdom. In fact, the ego is the biggest burden to itself, and thus relying too much on the ego's judgment is like living like a heavily laden ship. It is one's misbelief that the seemingly consistent but actually inconsistent and false ego is one's true self. Literature unlocks the Transmiddle Zone for us. As we desert the egoic identity, we enter the dimension of genuine *freedom* and *infinity*.

In addition, before addressing some literary works, I would first like to very briefly explain "affect theory," investigating why the theory's most representative point lies in Deleuze and Guattari's thought of "pure becoming." Above all, the reader can begin to think about the concept of ordinary becoming. However, if you experience what takes place inside you and call it "becoming," it is not an external process by which something changes into something other. Nor is it just an emotional change of the image you have into a better or worse one. *While reading a literary text or watching a film, following the story, and becoming immersed in the mood, you experience "becoming" the most important figure in the story.* The figure does not have to be a person; it can be an animal like a cat or a rat. Every kind of becoming, including "becoming-animal" (in Deleuze and Guattari's terms), is an artistic way of leading the reader or viewer from their uninteresting daily life to reach the dimension of the newness and purity that is beyond the concepts of pure and impure. Every becoming you experience while reading or watching is this way of later reaching a new dimension through subtle yet deeply strong effects of *imperceptible affect*.

In short, *pure becoming* cannot be shown in representational ways by thinking and language, but it is the most substantial power of all kinds of becoming. Pure becoming is a way of becoming the purest and reaching the deepest layer of being. It goes on in the realm of *affect*, not just in emotion. In actuality, everything grows older and changes each moment. Our thinking and feelings are always changing and becoming something else. The power and rhythm of the ever-ongoing changes and movements happen in the inmost depths of the existence that is even deeper than ordinary feelings. In other words, while ordinary feelings—happiness, anger, jealousy, etc.—are rough, phenomenal emotions, becoming is subtle, yet has the power of a strong impact that takes place on a deeper level than phenomena.

From this perspective, I would explore affect or *affectus* as the zone of imperceptible movement between emotion and the true self. In fact, I believe it is a very good situation that affect theory has been becoming increasingly popular in the English literature world in recent years, and I hope that deep layer of emotion and reason will be further discussed and revealed. As defined so far, *affectus* is the fundamental natural flow of the capacity to affect and be affected that goes on in a deeper layer than affection or *affectio* as emotion. Emotions are only the aquifer of affective states—the states of emotions and feelings such as pleasure, happiness, joy, sorrow, sadness, pain, fear, hate, and the like. Those raw emotions cannot break the shell of the ego in the form of binary opposition and reach Emptiness. Surely, Emptiness (or stillness) is not only in a peaceful and quiet situation but in the middle of a bustling roughness as well, while the roughness is unable to confront the most profound dimension. In sheer reality, weakness is stronger than corporeal strength. In this light, affect is the sensibility that transcends us, the readers, beyond the possibility of intellectual interpretation.

4.2. *Hamlet* as a long *kongan*

For both general readers and specialists in literature and film (e.g. critics), I would like to consider William Shakespeare's play, *Hamlet,* arguably the most well-known masterpiece in English literature. We will apply the Vipassana in the Theravada tradition first, and then keyword meditation (*hwadu-seon/ghanhwa-seon*) and silent illumination in the Ch'an (Chinese), Seon (Korean), and Zen (Japanese and generally acknowledged) traditions. Contemplative/centering prayer in the Christian religion could be included as well. All of these seemingly different styles of meditation lead us to encounter the same goal. *Hamlet* is one of the supreme examples of artworks that guide us, readers or viewers, to the ultimate reality, Emptiness, or the true self through the sublime sensibility. The sublime is the aesthetic way of reaching that frame of mind.

To begin with, all kinds of themes in *Hamlet* have always arisen from the fact that Hamlet is always *indeterminately* in the middle between the two polar opposites. First, he wants to avenge his father, the late king, by killing the current one, Claudius. Claudius is his father's younger brother, who murdered his father by pouring poison into his ear. Claudius also took Hamlet's mother as his wife after he became king. Hamlet does not avenge his father instantly after his father's ghost appeared and asked him to. Nor does he act upon the revenge after he came to be convinced of Claudius' killing of his father by seeing how Claudius responded to a play about a murder. Hamlet does not choose between the polar opposites.

Hamlet's hesitant, indeterminate mind is well-presented in the famous "To be, or not to be, that is the question" monologue in Act III, Scene 1. I propose that while immersed in reading or watching *Hamlet,* we experience the middle zone and unknowingly approach the true self.

Vipassana, or insightful meditation-style reading, is a way of understanding and accepting what is going on in a given story as it is, rather than laying our personal opinion upon it. The original meaning of Vipassana is simply the way of acknowledging and accepting what is happening at the present moment; it is not any type of meditation involving concentration on the body or its feelings. Vipassana meditation leads us to the light of *Bhodhi,* the true *wisdom* that lies beyond those phenomena. Reading in the Vipassana style, you will observe and accept the events and incidents that are narrated in the given story simply as they are described to you. Profound wisdom does not come from reasoning but from entirely accepting what you read in the mood of the given literary work. Do not interpret the story with any theme, but simply follow it as events happen. Of course, you will immediately start interpreting it when you read the story. Yet as you try to read without depending upon any possible theme that seems to be fixed in the story, it leads you to Emptiness without conceptual understanding, and that is what I call a Vipassana style of reading. Emptiness is the ultimate reality, and the Vipassana style of reading aims to encounter it.

In this light, it is important that in *Hamlet,* what is truly important is not the possible theme or fact that Hamlet has an indecisive nature, being irresolute about his duty of avenging his father. Yes, the whole story consists of Hamlet's hesitancy over his father. However, it does not simply mean that *Hamlet* the drama just indicates Hamlet's indecisive nature. Hamlet the main character's position in the middle zone between carrying out the task of avenging his father or not drives the reader's mind to

Emptiness, which is the dimension that always transcends life and death, presence and absence. We should be keenly aware that the space of true wisdom is not simply the middle. In fact, the deepening story leads us to both accept and exclude the polar opposites. To find true wisdom through *Hamlet* is to observe how the work deconstructs the binary structure so that it shows us that the middle zone is actually *limitless*. It indicates the zone of *infinity* between the polar opposites that forms the phenomenal binary structure. More precisely, it reveals the truth of the ego construct of humanity in general—individual and community. The truth is rather in contradiction to the dual nature of phenomena. In a more direct link to us, as readers and viewers, Hamlet's agony exposes what lies beyond his individual struggle—that is, the human psychic problems that are caused in the sequence of time and space.

Therefore, it is essential that we accept, perfectly and unreservedly, that *Hamlet* offers us an opportunity to glimpse the true transcendence, or Emptiness, that lies beyond and at the core of the phenomenal (binary opposition form) of the great existential anxiety. To put it differently, the genuine *wisdom* of you, the reader or viewer, does *not* take the *phenomenal form* of his decision of whether or not to avenge his father. The genuine, true wisdom comes from beneath the cause of Hamlet's hesitancy or any possibility of building a totality of the play. Hamlet's hesitancy, which has been taken up as the main idea of the work, is just an aged issue.

What *Hamlet* really presents to us is the profundity of the dual structure of existence. Hamlet's hesitancy and deep anxiety mean that he is seriously caught up in the net of the binary opposition. The opposition is formed by his weakness and cowardice of living ("to be") under Claudius' power and his duty of avenging his father ("not to be"). The middle zone between life and death cannot be described in language, and thus Hamlet's hesitation and agony regarding the avenging of his father is only what appears on the level of language. Shakespeare is certainly a great author, but I would say that he would not have known the depth of what he was writing—at least not on the conscious level! But the language of the play guides us, the readers, to the transcendental zone through the story, and then, at the end, lets us go beyond the language of the play itself. Let us consider perhaps the most famous monologue in English literature:

> To be, or not to be—that is the question:
> Whether 'tis nobler in the mind to suffer
> The slings and arrows of outrageous fortune
> Or to take arms against a sea of troubles
> And by opposing end them.
> To die, to sleep—

No more—and by a sleep to say we end
The heartache, and the thousand natural shocks
That flesh is heir to. 'Tis a consummation
Devoutly to be wished. To die, to sleep—
To sleep—perchance to dream: ay, there's the rub,
For in that sleep of death what dreams may come
When we have shuffled off this mortal coil,
Must give us pause. There's the respect
That makes calamity of so long life.
For who would bear the whips and scorns of time,
Th' oppressor's wrong, the proud man's contumely
The pangs of despised love, the law's delay,
The insolence of office, and the spurns
That patient merit of th' unworthy takes,
When he himself might his quietus make
With a bare bodkin? Who would fardels bear,
To grunt and sweat under a weary life,
But that the dread of something after death,
The undiscovered country, from whose bourn
No traveller returns, puzzles the will,
And makes us rather bear those ills we have
Than fly to others that we know not of?
Thus conscience does make cowards of us all,
And thus the native hue of resolution
Is sicklied o'er with the pale cast of thought,
And enterprise of great pitch and moment
With this regard their currents turn awry
And lose the name of action.
(Act III, Scene 1, 55-87)

Of the many film versions of *Hamlet,* the one directed by and starring
Kenneth Branagh (1996) is the most impressive to me. The "To be, or not
to be" scene is truly fabulous! There are many mirrors in the room Hamlet
enters, and behind the mirror he chooses (supposedly not consciously
chosen by Hamlet himself), Claudius and his subject, Polonius, are looking
at him from behind the two-way mirror. The presence of Claudius and
Polonius is unique to this movie. It is neither in the original nor in other film
or stage performances.

Here, the famous sentence "To be or not to be—that is the question" that
opens the monologue should be interpreted as "Not to avenge my father and
live in a cowardly way under Claudius' power or to avenge him and die
(because it would result in my death)." Throughout the whole play, Hamlet
is very indecisive and hesitant, stuck in the middle zone between the
resolutions until the last *tragic* moment where all figures are killed and

nothing about the issue is left. Then the play shows that Hamlet has missed his chances to kill Claudius' subject, Polonius, and Claudius himself. The existential question "To be, or not to be" separates the two fundamental issues that we all as humans have—living and dying—and then it starts to broaden the middle zone. This issue is the most profound and the ultimate question about life and death as a whole, since it means "Why do I exist?" or, in a more Buddhist view, "What makes me exist?"

Let us think about the monologue and the whole play again in this light. I would say that on the basic level, whether Hamlet succeeds in avenging his father is not important. The play as a whole guides us, the audience, to the most profound grounds of humanity. From the perspective of Buddhist spiritual pursuit, the whole drama is a vast *kongan,* and its *hwadu* should be one in direct relation to "To be or not to be?" It should be some question that directs us to what constructs the duality of life and the root of the dual nature of humanity.

The following is another of Hamlet's soliloquies, in which he seems to be firmly determined to avenge his father:

> How all occasions do inform against me,
> And spur my dull revenge! What is a man,
> If his chief good and market of his time
> Be but to sleep and feed? a beast, no more.
> Sure, he that made us with such large discourse,
> Looking before and after, gave us not
> That capability and god-like reason
> To fust in us unused. Now, whether it be
> Bestial oblivion, or some craven scruple
> Of thinking too precisely on the event,
> A thought which, quarter'd, hath but one part wisdom
> And ever three parts coward, I do not know
> Why yet I live to say 'This thing's to do;'
> Sith I have cause and will and strength and means
> To do't. Examples gross as earth exhort me:
> Witness this army of such mass and charge
> Led by a delicate and tender prince,
> Whose spirit with divine ambition puff'd
> Makes mouths at the invisible event,
> Exposing what is mortal and unsure
> To all that fortune, death and danger dare,
> Even for an egg-shell. Rightly to be great
> Is not to stir without great argument,
> But greatly to find quarrel in a straw
> When honour's at the stake. How stand I then,
> That have a father kill'd, a mother stain'd,

Excitements of my reason and my blood,
And let all sleep? while, to my shame, I see
The imminent death of twenty thousand men,
That, for a fantasy and trick of fame,
Go to their graves like beds, fight for a plot
Whereon the numbers cannot try the cause,
Which is not tomb enough and continent
To hide the slain? O, from this time forth, My thoughts be bloody, or be
nothing worth!
(Act IV, Scene 4, 35-69)

However, Hamlet does not go on to kill the king, and the story of his weakness continues. The whole of *Hamlet* comprises his indetermination, vacillation, and delay in avenging his father. The story leads the reader through his irresolution and hesitation between killing and surviving. This means that the play directs our attention to the deepest level that cannot be described in language—the Transmiddle Zone. Again, whether Hamlet succeeds in avenging his father is not really important for us. The reader is led through the flux happening between the two opposites.

At the end, Hamlet attains justice for the death of his father, but at the cost of his life. Both Hamlet and Claudius are killed by each other. Hamlet's mother also dies. Laertes kills Hamlet with a poisoned sword in a fencing fight and dies declaring that he is justly killed for his own treachery: he tells Hamlet that he, too, has been slain, by his own poisoned sword, and that the king is to blame both for the poison on the sword and for the poison in the cup. All important figures on both Hamlet's side and Claudius' side are killed, and no one is left. Breathing his last breath, Hamlet tells Horatio that he is dying and urges him not to commit suicide in this tragic situation and to stay alive and tell his story to others. He says that he wishes Fortinbras to be made King of Denmark, then he dies. At the last tragic moment, everything is blown up, and neither of the two sides remain (Act V, Scene 2). The final words that Hamlet himself says are "Rest is silence," and the reader is left in a state of stillness. This silence is not the silence we meet at the last moment of living. Through stillness, the reader can experience a glimpse of what lies beyond language—Emptiness and infinity.

It is not my purpose to attach a meaning to this ending of *Hamlet* by interpreting it within a thematic approach. In contrast to the traditional way of interpreting a literary piece with meanings and an all-embracing theme, I would highlight what sublime effect the end of this drama has left on the hearts of innumerable people of the world throughout the centuries. The ending of such a tragic story as this breaks open our mind beyond all conflicts that are ontological and perceivable. This is the real moment when we practice meditating on what happens in the dimension of invisibility. Like the goal of *kongans* and *hwadus* in meditation, the goal of a literary text is to lead us above and beyond human thought by showing the destruction of its own structure. It points to the realm where "I think, therefore I am" is never a principle. The text simply shows the devastation of Yin and Yang, the polar opposites. No victory of either one, no reflection, no value judgment is left.

The story is, after all, not your own story, and thus you as the reader are not experiencing the incidents and events taking place in the story too vividly. After observing the whole story and mood as a *kongan,* the *hwadu* you would have is, "What is this?" More accurately, the *hwadu* is, "What is in the middle (center) of the opposites that constitute human decisions?" Or simply, "What is the true, infinite self?" Then, as Hamlet says at the end of the drama when breathing his last, "The rest is silence." Dualism and delusion caused by the ego disappear. It is critical that, just as a Ch'an/Seon/Zen master does not explain or give the answer to *kongans* and *hwadus,* the text leaves us with silence.

In the conclusion of the story, duality finally collapses, but it collapses without a real solution or a pleasurable result of the long-lasting and enhanced problem. Tragedies are characteristic of breaking the dual structure of the story without an actual ontological solution. All that the textual language describes can never escape the circuit of the binary construct of the egoistic nature of individuals, groups, and society. Tragic stories consist of complicated plots that evoke the emotions of jealousy, anger, and sympathy from us, the readers.

In this light, *Hamlet* as a whole is like a vast *kongan* in Ch'an/Seon/Zen Buddhism, and the ending works like the well-known Buddhist image of a finger directing our mind toward the moon. The deconstruction of the two extremes—happiness and pain—has been completed. And because the story is not your own, you may feel *apathy* or *indifference,* the last phase of the sublime, while or after undergoing emotional states. Both in meditation and in the sublime, the ultimate *hwadu* makes us search for what transcends. However, the literary work or film would lead you to the fact that life is like a dream, in which everything is transient and vain, and that the dreamer is your real self, the imperceptible, universal, infinite Truth itself, called "Emptiness with wondrous movement" or simply "Emptiness" in Mahayana Buddhism.

Phenomena are important to us, yet they are only the appearances of the ultimate reality, which always eludes our perception. We and all beings and objects are manifestations of the true reality. I do not mean that the dimension of truth is somewhere else than our mundane daily life. We can find the dimension of the ultimate reality (non-identified or non-signified) through the subtle sensibility that we experience in silence—either while immersed in meditation or contemplation or while experiencing the aesthetic sublime. The aesthetic experience of the sublime (otherwise called *jouissance*) that we go through as we read a literary text is very much like the meditative state of mind.

From the aesthetic point of view, the meditative state is the sublime moment in which we glimpse the ultimate reality, Emptiness. Emptiness necessarily brings *apathy* or *indifference* toward the presence of beings and things in life. Apathy is the last phase of the sublime while or after undergoing emotional states. Both in meditation and in the sublime, the ultimate *hwadu* makes us search for what transcends, yet within the heart of phenomenal emotion and reason. The sublime is a *spiritual* feeling.

While reading any given story, the reader should practice accepting both the side of pleasure and pain, beauty and the ugly side of life, as they are. Within the zone of sense perception, pain and suffering in reality are only other forms of pleasure. In the light of postmodern ethics and Buddhism, the ultimate reality is the exterior of the sphere of sense perception and intellectualization. More specifically, I would recommend that you experience the story and its mood not with a mind to find out the main message but just to accept and realize the *impermanence* of transient mental and physical phenomena arising and passing away.

You do not have to use any techniques to understand the story and accept the mood. If that literary work or film is one that is not simply for entertainment but aesthetically valid, it would already show you *dukkha*. *Dukkha* means "suffering" or "pain" caused by the nature of "unsatisfactoriness" of human desire. It is a common word in Vipassana/insight meditation and Ch'an/Seon/Zen meditation. The *hwadus* of the keyword meditation represented by the question would guide you directly to the final goal of the literary work or film. "What is this?" is a question to quest for the ultimate cause and goal of the whole artwork. All these thoughts in postmodern critical theory or Buddhist traditions share the same point that true wisdom comes from the exterior of the ego. This spirituality is what readers and viewers come to attain while reading. In this way, religious experience and aesthetic appreciation should go together, as I have been explaining since the beginning of this book.

Concerning the issue of how we appreciate literature and film and practice criticism, I have come to employ the merits of both traditions, Vipassana and Zen, to develop the theory of the sublime, particularly the postmodern sublime. The real sense of the postmodern sublime that contemporary thinkers such as Emmanuel Levinas, Jean-François Lyotard,

Jean-Luc Nancy, and others elaborate on is more of a spiritual feeling than what Kant explains in the *Critique of Judgment,* his third critique after the *Critique of Pure Reason* and the *Critique of Practical Reason.* From the postmodern perspective, the sublime feeling that detaches one's true self from the ego, or the false self, is more radically liberal than the Kantian notion of the sublime. It deserves the name "the postmodern sublime," an even freer feeling of spirituality than the notion of the sublime explained by Kant.

Kant does not account for the universal (more than great and maximum) sense of a state of the subjective mind in great detail. I regard the aesthetic sublime as a much more spiritual experience. The best book on the postmodernist elaboration of Kantian thought of the sublime is *Of the Sublime*,[35] which offers us the thoughts of Nancy and Lyotard. In fact, the idea of the sublime is not so unfamiliar to the public. "The sublime" is thought of as being one with the simple meaning of having the best pleasure. But the sublime is not merely something that is so nice or beautiful to look at that you are deeply moved by it. It is a transcendental, spiritual feeling.

In connection with the sublime, an idea of Wolfgang Iser, a reader-response critic, will help you understand this kind of state of deepening spiritual and ethical as well as aesthetic feelings—especially at the end of the reading. What other reader-response critics call the "real" reader, Iser calls an "implied" reader, who is the one that a given literary work requires. For example, those who become immersed in reading Edgar Allan Poe's Gothic-style poems and short stories are suggested to follow the author's intent to shock and thrill them. Yet it is important to notice that the reader comes to take the role of *feeling* this way—whatever tension they have between their own historical daily reality and reading the artwork. However, in any case, the reader is not quite ready to accept the given ideas or a theme that totalizes the text.[36] An implied reader is not one who is easily imbued with a totalizing ideology, political idea, or any other ideology. As Gilles Deleuze and Felix Guattari (1930-92) say in *A Thousand Plateaus*, "There is no ideology and never has been."[37]

I agree with Iser that the literary text is not just an object to be interpreted by the reader in any way. Through the details of characters and settings, the

[35] Rodolphe Gasche and Mark C. Taylor, eds., *Of the Sublime: Presence in Question,* trans. Jeffrey S. Librett (Albany: State University of New York Press, 1993).
[36] Wolfgang Iser, *The Act of Reading: A Theory of Aesthetic Response* (Baltimore: Johns Hopkins University Press, 1978), 35.
[37] Gilles Deleuze and Felix Guattari, *A Thousand Plateaus: Capitalism and Schizophrenia,* trans. Brian Massumi (Minneapolis: University of Minnesota Press, 1987), 4.

implied reader is led to the Transmiddle way, beyond the polarities of binary opposites and multiplication. Through a "wandering viewpoint," the reader is expected to see that the ultimate reality of life is not abstraction or phenomena but genuine Emptiness—genuine stillness with wondrous movement. It would be very awkward and wrong if you read Poe's short stories while considering they were written simply to shock and horrify you. Poe does not seem to have any goal. Putting you in a shocking and grotesque mood does not have the purpose of making you fear the unknown or the unknowable—the wholly other of the ego.

Such an attitude is never *post*modern. As Lyotard affirms, postmodernism is essentially postmodern ethics! Postmodern ethics is never a set of moral rules. Since the time of Kant, and in this age of postmodern ethics, ethics rather entirely destroys any form of moral, political, or even aesthetic forms. These forms could be supposed to bring us to the transcendental dimension beyond the reality of everyday life. A set of moral rules conditions people's minds and lives, and those rules would be pejorative toward others who do not observe those rules. In political situations, egoic political rulers and social dominators take advantage of morality. For example, the issue of prohibiting killing is of primary importance not only in Christianity and Buddhism but in all other major religions. However, the issue should be interpreted literally and applied to all situations. In war, it is beyond question that you are to kill the enemy. Otherwise, you will get killed. In the Second World War, the moral issues of Nazi Germany, Fascist Italy, and Imperial Japan were all for the sake of the dictators themselves and their followers.

Nevertheless, first and foremost, the "no killing" issue is a universal issue common to all human systems and the most fundamental standard in Eastern and Western philosophies, spiritual thoughts, and all major religions. Now, let us inquire more about the sublime in detail regarding Buddhism. Does it not have the power to provide a breakthrough to Emptiness? In fact, there would be some unclear understanding and questionable points if you applied Vipassana directly to literary reading. It would be especially so as you would place yourself in the middle or Transmiddle way. Yet the truly significant point is that Vipassana means becoming clearly aware of what you are doing. There is much for reading techniques in Vipassana, except that it would make you feel more clearly or more intensively.

Much more than Vipassana, as I explained in the last chapter, the Buddhist Ch'an/Seon/Zen traditions would be more effectively employed in confirming how the reading of literary texts is by nature very similar to their ways of meditation or contemplation. In Seon Buddhism, "sitting meditation" with *kongan* questions (a *kongan* is a very short dialogue or anecdote that arouses a strong curiosity and desire to know the ultimate reality in the mind of a meditator) and *hwadus* (keywords) are the main techniques for attaining a breakthrough to the perfect emptiness. From the perspective of Korean Seon Buddhism, as the reader experiences enjoyment (*jouissance*) and the broader sense of the sublime, they are detached from any decision on the lasting totality of perception. The special point should be laid on the ending of a literary story. The reader is led to find the middle way between the opposite poles that constitute the thought, and they reach beyond presence and absence. At last, the reader glimpses the other, or the real self beyond language, and this means that the pure I, or "the real I," is absolutely beyond or outside the circuit of the usually understood, empirical, or impure I.

After reading or watching the whole story, you can start meditating on the issue of Emptiness. *Hamlet* is set on the stage of the dichotomy formed by Hamlet and Claudius, both of whom die at the end. The drama ends without a phenomenal victory of one side over the other. Literature ushers us to the door to the realm of true freedom from binary opposition. The door is open to the dimension of the middle zone between the primarily opposed two different aspects of the human subject that produce the perception of phenomena.

Silent meditation would help you to go on to deeply feel that *there is no actual distinction between good and evil.* To put it in other words, *Hamlet is Claudius, Claudius is Hamlet!* Good and evil personalities are just conditioned phenomena. Phenomenally, it would seem to be only natural that we like pleasure and happiness and avoid suffering. Yet this nature of pursuing pleasure and happiness brings about conflicts between individuals in a society and between different nations. However, these are all dream-like contexts of our lives and human history. All events are conditioned by our own individual, separate personalities and relations with others, and beyond, or behind, those egoic feelings and events based upon them, or within the heart of them (producing them), we are all one!

All other characters in the drama are, on the most profound level of being and non-being, one. There is only the wondrous movement of Emptiness. The movement of Emptiness produces and destroys every being in the whole universe. As you realize that the ultimate reality is Emptiness, you would start to have tranquil and undisturbed feelings of bliss. It is the feeling of the sublime, or *jouissance*, through which your mind transcends the level of egoic feelings such as anger, jealousy, anxiety, love as the feeling of being attached to an outside object, and hate.

At the end of *Hamlet, neither Hamlet nor Claudius defeats the other*. Only Hamlet's words to Horatio to tell his story to people of the future let us have some feeling that his good nature and the justice he has attained will last. But such a hope would not produce any stable, unchangeable theme of the drama. The conclusion of *Hamlet* lets us, the readers, experience the dimension of life deeper than the ontological surface of life. It shows the total destruction of the egoistic desire to keep everlasting youth as opposed to aging. It means the debacle of another form of binary opposition.

In this light, the goal of literature and film leads us to reach the source of the movement of infinity through what Kant calls "subjective univocity." The sublime feeling is subjective, but that feeling is one with the whole of all beings and non-beings. This sensibility can never be described or conveyed through the "meaning" of language and scenes—that is, *not* through a thematic approach to language. It leads us beyond ideology to the truly (not relatively but absolutely) pure, universal consciousness. After all, both Buddhism and literature/film reveal that life as such, whether it appears to be pleasurable or displeasurable, is *dukkha*—insufficiency that causes suffering.

What matters is humans' phenomenal desire for more, which Levinas and Lacan call "need," not a real metaphysical desire for infinity. The meditative state we experience after reading or watching the whole drama of *Hamlet* is the primary sphere of humanity or being with no intensity of wish. Literature and the arts lead us to this fundamentality of life with no phenomenal intensity of existence. Beautiful works of art are means to release the intensity of the emotions that opens the gate to transcendence, the imperceptible movement of infinity, through the sublime sensibility.

While you understand and experience Hamlet's and Claudius' thoughts and feelings, in Deleuze and Guattari's terms, you are *becoming* Hamlet, and it means that you experience *becoming pure and imperceptible* through the images of the objects. *Pure becoming* is reaching the center of life that is empty of any phenomenal movement, and while you experience it, you are detached from the structure of the binary opposition. You come to glimpse the infinity of the heterogeneous other of the self. In this way, you come to reach the exteriority of subjectivity/self where there is no egoic dual vision—right and wrong, happiness and fear, love and hatred. That is the beginning of all discernment and reason. It is especially noticeable that, as Deleuze and Guattari declare, literature is "an assemblage. It has nothing to do with ideology. There is no ideology and never has been."[38] The deaths of all the people in Hamlet, including Claudius and Hamlet himself, prove it.

That is to say, ideology as any big or small system of conceptual thoughts is dead, and literature and film guide us beyond the realm of forms. A

---

[38] Deleuze and Guattari, *A Thousand Plateaus*, 4.

literary reading is like Jesus' calling of Lazarus from the dead: "Lazarus, come forth!" (John 11:38). Literature and film guide us to the true source of life that lies beyond the seemingly stable meaning generated by language. A literary work or a film is just a body of many signs and possible themes, creeds, or dogmas, and its purpose is to lead the audience beyond itself as a work of language and scenes.

As a work is interpreted with any possible theme by audiences, both the signs and the theme are merely dead images; there is no real life in the phenomenal ideas, which are not really moving but fixed. The power of life comes from the part of the reader's mind that is rather meaningless. If one encounters literature and film from this new perspective of postmodern ethics, the audiences would repudiate the traditional way of interpreting the story with a possible moral theme with proper reason that seems to justify the interpretation. Instead, they would acknowledge the inner aim of the text to remove the shell of human egoic (dualistically structured) power disguised with reason and logic.

The possibility of the thematic approach is still valid to offer the audience only some knowledge of the cultural environment that the author or the movie was placed in. However, the thematic possibility should take one of the elements of the existence of an artwork and not more than that. Literature and film are not stores of cultural information. As a warehouse of pieces of intellectual understanding, newspapers and magazines of the specific age and society must be much better sources. It is very clear to me that the final goal of literature and film as art is to guide us to univocity, and it is definitely not to end up producing transient meanings and short-lasting ideology. Think about communism. However ideal an ideology it seemed, many literary works such as George Orwell's *Animal Farm* and others that praise communism were short-lived. As long as it celebrates an ideology, I think, it has no worth other than propaganda. A propaganda novel, poem, drama, or film is not art! The ultimate purpose of serious literary works and films is to reach the enduring, unchanging, and undecidable exterior that both transcends and ontologically produces phenomena.

In this way, literature never gets entangled with a thematic approach, for it leads the reader beyond the human decision-making faculty. As you practice meditation with *hwadu,* as I suggested above, after reading a text or viewing a film adaptation, you will approach the dimension of non-duality where you are not a separate entity from what you see in your daily life. Moreover, you are not separate from the absolute truth because it is your real self. That is to say, all are phenomenally different, yet fundamentally one. That is why one of the most important points to notice in Mahayana

Buddhism is "not one, but not two." "Not one, but not two" is the Buddha-nature that I call the "Transmiddle Path" in this book.

4.3. *Moby-Dick* as a vast *kongan*: Affect and literature

I would like to connect the issues of *affect* and *becoming* that are mainly used by Deleuze and Guattari to a reading of a literary text at this point. All kinds of *becoming* we experience while reading literary works or watching films are pure becoming or becoming pure, that is, coming to be one with infinity. What I mean by infinity is the same as what Levinas means and also what has been studied and quested for in Buddhism.

Particularly the *concluding* part of a literary work or film leaves a great impact on us. The whole story first provides us with opportunities to open our mind at the deepest level and glimpse the infinite movement and the vast and limitlessly varying form of the other (non-phenomenal movement outside the ego). After the whole narrative, the *ending* drives us finally to experience our true selves through the special sensibility of the sublime. The sublime sensibility paves a way toward the movement of the infinite. The final goal is neither any reasoned result nor any emotional situation. The purpose of the way for us to reach is *imperceptible affect,* not a perceptible subjective view or theme that has taken its form in our perceiving and discerning mind.

In this way, the ending of a story lets us directly confront the other. I do not mean you can feel sublimity only at the end of a story. Yet, the true nature of the particular (usually tragic) situation at the end, through which the wholly other of your ego reveals its face, is the straightforward way of the *sublimity* of the work of art. The conclusion of a masterpiece drives us, the readers, to face the sublime state directly, without the mask that hides it, and become immersed in it. The sublime replaces all possible themes that take place in the realms of perception and conceptualization.

Your true self is not the small, separate, individual ego, what you think you are as a small cognizable entity that understands literary works and movies only with a seemingly set theme or main message. In contrast, it is the true self of all humans and the universe. Your true self is the infinite universal movement, flow, or flux of the universe as a body without organs that is becoming infinity itself. The true self is Emptiness itself, void of egoic desire. The artwork is an example of what can be called the divine play or the dance of God, as is called "Lila" in Hinduism.

One of the supreme examples we can take in connection with Deleuze and Guattari's terms of becoming, affect, and the body without organs is *Moby-Dick; or, The Whale,* one of the greatest American novels ever.

"*Moby-Dick* in its entirety is one of the greatest masterpieces of becoming; Captain Ahab has an irresistible becoming-whale ... operating directly through a monstrous alliance with the Unique, the Leviathan, Moby Dick."[39] *Moby-Dick* was written by Herman Melville (1819-1891), who is now known as one of the greatest American novelists, and published in 1851. There have since been film adaptations in the U.S.—including in 1926 and 1956, and a TV miniseries in 1998 (*In the Heart of the Sea*, a movie released in 2015, is based on the story of the real event that inspired Melville's novel). The recent Canadian-German TV miniseries produced in 2011 as a two-part film heightens the dramatic effect with a long running time (3 hours and 11 minutes). It succeeds in portraying Captain Ahab as an obsessed but rather warm-hearted man, unlike the image of Ahab in the 1956 film. The repeated remaking of the novel reflects that it indeed powerfully touches the heart of the audience, and the power, without doubt, comes from its intense sublimity. The film adaptations are tremendously faithful to the original and offer astonishing sublimity to the audience.

Melville's novel is the story of Captain Ahab's attempt to seek his revenge on Moby Dick, a huge whale.[40] As a very short synopsis of the long story, Ahab's left leg was bitten by Moby Dick, and Ahab thereafter burned with an immense and deep-seated desire for revenge on the monstrously big whale. The sole purpose of his navigation is to kill the whale following him across the oceans. In the end, while the obsessed Ahab and his crew chase Moby Dick, the wounded whale attacks and wrecks Ahab's ship, named "Pequod," and kills all the crew except for Ishmael, who survives and narrates this story. In his last attack, Ahab comes to be entangled in the hemp rope attached to the harpoon and is pulled into the sea. Without question, he dies with the whale he always wished to conquer.

At the level of appearances, Ahab destroys both himself and Moby Dick. However, from our perspective, throughout the whole narrative and especially in the *conclusion*, Ahab *becomes* Moby Dick. Moby Dick should not be considered only as Ahab's target of revenge. Moby Dick is symbolic of the most profoundly enigmatic object of our life—God—in terms of identity. Yet it can be called by other names for truth—the whole, the Real, Buddha-nature, infinity, Emptiness. In *Moby-Dick,* it takes the form of the whale as the object of Ahab's revenge. What is most important is that you, as a reader or viewer, follow the story and also become like Ahab and, finally, *become* Moby Dick through the sublime sensibility.

Captain Ahab's story halts the flow of your egoic mind and drives you to what he thinks of as the most important target for his life. His target, the

---

[39] Deleuze and Guattari, *A Thousand Plateaus*, 243.
[40] Herman Melville, *Moby-Dick* (New York: Signet Classics, 2013).

whale, is what is wholly other than his ego, or the other of his ego. It is the fundamental source of life itself. Then, in the end, the duality of Ahab's egoic construct that consists of himself and his target is destroyed, and there is only one world, which is out of reach of your understanding. In the last scene of the novel, both Ahab (together with his crew) and the whale are placed in a situation in which they die. When the whale returns to Ahab, who stabs it again, Ahab gets tangled with the line looping around his neck and disappears with Moby Dick out of sight, drowning. Ishmael is the only survivor who is rescued. He is the one who can tell Ahab's story of his ambition to conquer such a big whale. He is like Horatio, who is to tell Hamlet's story in the future. (Hamlet asks him to do so.) However, Horatio is only a figure in the story, while Ishmael is actually the narrator of the novel.

I would like to bring to light that Moby Dick embodies Ahab's innermost desire for his true self in the form of his fear of it. Fear is one of the most representative motives in literature and film. For Ahab, the huge, monstrous whale is just the object of his vengeance with an enormous amount of anger. If it were not so, this novel would not impact the reader so powerfully. What would be the purpose of writing this kind of novel and reading it? Ahab's pursuit of the whale rather embodies his gigantic desire for becoming one with this most enigmatic object. The most profoundly abstruse and mysterious object that cannot be described with language is the spiritual realm of the universal, true self.

It is the ultimate reality that makes this work leave such an imperceptible but enduring chord with the reader. Of course, such a strong impact would not be possible if it were described only on the level of symbols and metaphors. The process by which Ahab becomes Moby Dick drives us to the level of affect where we encounter the most profound level of life and death in one form. In any case, I would say the most crucial point is that we, with Ahab, experience the momentum to break through the line of becoming pure beyond the language of the novel itself, and that we as readers follow the same goal while being immersed in reading the novel and experiencing the sublime, especially at the end of the story.

In other words, throughout the story, the reader's process of becoming Moby Dick means that they open toward the exterior of the ego and come to encounter the true self. Moby Dick is the emblem of the reader's true self that they themselves are not consciously aware of. The novel provides us with one of the greatest literary moments of facing the true face of ourselves—not in a collective (social, cultural) sense but the very nature of us both individually and collectively! Thus, to Ahab, Moby Dick is an embodiment of the universal true self, and what is much more, the reader experiences facing, encountering, and *becoming* their true self. The supreme sublime scene is the last one.

It is right to say that, in this novel, Ahab "enters a zone of indiscernibility where he can no longer distinguish himself from Moby-Dick, to the point where he strikes himself in striking the whale," and so do you, the reader.[41] It is done in a generally *grotesque* Gothic mood that attracts you. Moby Dick is an emblem of the other of Captain Ahab's individual, small mind. Ahab's separate mind, his ego, is extremely and fervently obsessed with the huge whale. Yet it is a surface value. It does not seem to me that Ahab is merely obsessed with the matter of having his revenge on an animal. I propose that, in its depths, his egoic mind is *obsessed with true liberty from itself!* Externally, he desires to kill the whale that destroyed his left leg. Yet it really means that he wants to free himself from his ego. He desires to encounter the other and become one with it. By this process, on the level of sublime sensibility, he *becomes the imperceptible other, and so do you.*

Now, maybe you are nodding in agreement just because Ahab pursues the whale and becomes one with it in the end. Yes, the outward appearance of the story appears so. Nonetheless, I do not simply mean that the novel works this way symbolically. I mean that you may truly agree with me when you experience glimpsing the exterior of your mind for yourself. Especially as a literary reader, you can agree with me in a different way. Yes. Examine what you feel while reading the novel, and at the end in particular. What do you feel after you finish reading the whole novel? Do you really feel like figuring out what the novel's message is in its language? Or do you feel something else than defining a possible theme of the novel?

I am convinced that if the novel is an artwork, it must leave something else than its theme with the audience, something that not only synthesizes the whole story as a conceptualization. Conceptualization is trying to interpret the story by categorizing it by forming a concept. Yet when you follow the story, behind what you grasp by unifying some ideas and separating others from them, there are true realities where those ideas are possible. That genuine, not fleeting, yet *imperceptible* reality is the ultimate reality of all our lives. Literature as an artwork opens your heart to that reality.

Ahab wishes to solve the greatest problem in his life, and he becomes free of the greatest riddle, dilemma, and mystery not by separating it from himself but by becoming one with it! The conclusion of the story stops your thinking and you may feel the sublime, by which you feel yourself being

---

[41] Daniel W. Smith, "Introduction: 'A Life of Pure Immanence': Deleuze's 'Critique et Clinique' Project," in Gilles Deleuze, *Essays Critical and Clinical*, trans. Daniel W. Smith and Michael A. Greco (Verso: London, 1998), xxx.

absorbed into the identity of the huge whale, Moby Dick. Or you may feel empty or indifferent because, after all, the story is not your own life story, and thus you would not have vividly *tragic* feelings. Because the goal is outside the knowledge accumulated in your egoic mind, you may well feel apathy. This apathy does not mean you are merely disinterested or dispassionate about the story. It means that you do not feel any strong emotion because you are faced with an ungraspable reality. It is ungraspable intellectually or emotionally, yet you may still experience the sensibility of encountering the ultimate reality. It goes beyond ordinary pleasure into the experience par excellence, the experience of infinity, the exterior of the self.[42]

It must be first understandable to you that, while reading the novel or watching one of the adapted films, you may experience *becoming* Moby Dick through Ahab on the level of understanding the symbols and metaphors that take place in the Gothic (eerie, mysterious, grotesque, lost security) mood and in Ahab's hatred for Moby Dick. But more deeply, the real mystery of Moby Dick unfolds on the level of affect or the excess of the Gothic mood. As explained earlier, affect comprises the impersonal, transpersonal, and immeasurable flow that takes place beyond the subject-object communication level. The excess of the Gothic mood is like the aura of that *grotesque* mood. In this literary space of this text, the whale is not only Ahab's but also your own object of immense desire to know the (non-phenomenal) unknowable in the outward way of describing it with symbols and metaphors. Affect or the sublime is possible only on the basis of which bodily sensation—and this is the way toward the ultimate reality—lies beyond the subject-object relation. In this way, reading as a becoming process leads us to experience the sublime as the excess of the Gothic mood that leads us beyond the ego function that consists of binary opposition. In this most profound level of affect or aura, your formless true self, in contradiction to the ego, finds its form in your half-/quasi-phenomenal existence of feelings and reasoning mind.

Explaining what is truly distinct from the mind-generated orders of its perception of phenomena outside of itself does not form ideas by conceptualizing the phenomena. Deleuze and Guattari also take "becoming-vampire" as an example of *becoming a heterogeneous, unknown other*. What they call "becoming-vampire" has nothing to do with some abstract idea or image of personas. They employ the term "infection" to describe the active and dynamic way of becoming-vampire. Literary reading is like becoming a vampire figure and influences the reader with the heterogeneous nature of the exterior of the self in the moods of terror, thrill, and loss of

---

[42] Lee, *Postmodern Ethics*, 86.

security. Infecting is imparting, conveying, or passing along to others, not through the process of sending ideas as separate units but in a condition like flowing liquid or blowing air. It is a way of becoming the other.

Becoming Moby Dick is also a process of "infection." As you read Ahab's story of revenge on the whale, you become overwhelmed by his strong will for revenge through the Gothic mood. You first become Ahab, and then Moby Dick. Just as in the case of reading *Moby-Dick,* the unknown object, you *become* Dracula, the evil object, and this means that the reader comes to confront the true self represented with the artistic form of Dracula. Of course, Dracula is pursued in a great deal more eerie and mysterious Gothic mood that arouses fear, shock, loss of security, and horror in the reader. Just as Dracula, the "undead" vampire, is an emblem of the unknown other, Moby Dick is an inhuman monster. At any rate, *Moby-Dick* and *Dracula* have the strong power of sublimity, which leads the reader beyond their language and the *grotesque* Gothic mood. The true self is perfect Emptiness beyond phenomena: it is what you can *be* (and use), but not something that you can perceive and think about.[43]

In fact, every becoming—becoming rat, becoming insect—is an infection or intermingling that is not being conceptually influenced and changed. It is not a work that a concept could accomplish. Becoming is a process of reaching outside the self/ego through a given figure, and it can be done only in terms of *affect*. Becoming or becoming pure is emptying the self through the given story and mood, which is being detached from the structure of binary opposition. Great works in literature and film, in various ways, offer us precious opportunities to encounter and *become* the universal and infinite true self. In the final chapter, I explore more literary texts and films with the sublimity that surpasses all the standards of our five senses.[44] In other words, the dimension of the ultimate reality pursued by literature and film is the realm of the liberated, true self, which is not graspable by the rough emotions arising from the ego, the prison-like finite self. The sublime is a way to free the reader and viewer. This experience remains in your heart

---

[43] For more on *Dracula,* see Lee, *Postmodern Ethics*, Chap. 6.

[44] In the history of Western metaphysics, the sublime, especially the Gothic sublime, has been studied by such thinkers as Cassius Longinus, Edmund Burke, and especially Immanuel Kant. In his *A Philosophical Enquiry into the Origin of our Ideas of the Sublime and Beautiful* (1757), Burke proclaimed that pain, loss of security, terror, and suffering are much more intense feelings than pleasure and that they are far more helpful to us as we try to open our mind to sublimity. Later, Kant, in his *Critique of Judgment*, confirmed and developed this idea and elaborated on the sublime in great detail.

and, later on, reminds you of your experience of the story. It makes you think about the depth of life even as time passes.

The 2011 Canadian-German miniseries *Moby Dick* starring William Hurt has a strong power. As a TV series, it takes longer to go into detail. It portrays Ahab's personality more closely than the 1956 Hollywood film starring Gregory Peck. It also draws out the conclusion beyond its previous length.

In addition, regarding the structure of a Gothic novel, Mary Shelley's *Frankenstein* is closer than Bram Stoker's *Dracula* to *Moby-Dick*. Victor Frankenstein introduces the (nameless) monster to the reader, just as Ahab introduces Moby Dick to you. Then you follow Frankenstein to become the monster, just as you follow Ahab to become Moby Dick. In all cases, monsters such as Frankenstein's creature and Count Dracula are emblems of the unknown other, just like Moby Dick.

Now, let us think more about how we meditate with this artwork. Artworks of a mediocre quality would not give the audience a great sublime impact. Yet canonized literary texts and great films are truly appreciated due to the superb effect of the sublime. Through the spiritual feeling of the sublime, you enter the dimension of the *imperceptible*. It is the path paved for you to the ultimate reality of yourself and the world. The sublime, for which another name could be *jouissance*, is the nucleus of the novel as an artwork. The spiritual feeling of the aesthetic sublime lies beyond your sense and emotion, yet you undoubtedly experience it. It is not your idea that Captain Ahab is foolish for wanting revenge on a whale, nor is it your admiration for his intense persistence. Beyond or behind all the possible ideas and themes, there lies a way in which the reason and emotions that produce them lie in indifference to them. Reasoning and ordinary kinds of emotion are necessary to bring the path toward the space of spirituality, but the postmodern sublime—not just Kant's notion of the sublime—perfectly negates the empirical results of experience for the sake of spirituality. What the postmodern sublime offers us is an even more inward feeling of spirituality that liberates us more than the notion of the sublime explained by Kant.

Thus, for you, the *hwadu* for the reading of *Moby-Dick* as a very long *kongan* should be a question that never allows the slightest certainty of empirical experience that is represented by a theme or main message from the novel. The *hwadu* would be: "Why is Ahab so obsessed with Moby Dick?", "What is it that Ahab desires to be one with?" or "What is it that attaches Ahab so intensely to Moby Dick that drives him to his destructive obsession?" All these questions come down to "What is Moby Dick really?"

This corresponds to the representational *hwadu* in Ch'an/Seon Buddhism, "What is this?"

After reading the whole novel, the sublime as the path of stillness toward the transcendental dimension of the other is, from the Buddhist perspective, akin to the state of "*Samadhi*." *Samadhi* is the deeply meditative state that is the way of encountering the real self. This state of mind is possible only when one is not attached to but rather detached from and transcending the dual form of the ego, which is the transitory and illusory self.

Of course, you may need a great deal of training to reach *Samadhi* or *Jhana*. Yet the path of stillness you enter right after you finish reading the novel could be the initial stage. It is the stage of *doubting* all empirical experience. You need a great doubt to gain momentum for the purest awareness itself. As your experience deepens, you come closer to the ultimate enlightenment. In fact, pure awareness is the source of the ego's perception. *It is the thinking ego that understands the literary story, but the ego's binary opposition dissolves in the power of the unthinking true self that appears in the Middle Path between the polar opposites.*

Please remain in this meditative state for a while. First of all, repeatedly ask yourself the *hwadu* from *Moby-Dick* as a vast *kongan*. Just think about what Moby Dick really is, or why Ahab is so obsessed with his revenge and dies with Moby Dick. There is no answer you can find. Our goal is the "don't-know mind," as mentioned in the previous chapter. After a while, let go of all thoughts about the novel.

Your true self is not a separate, individual self, which is your ego. No, it is not the ego. What is it that lets you move? What makes you think and feel? In brief, what is it/this? If a thought comes to your mind, do not try to expel it. Do not follow the image or words that came to you, either; do not bring it to your attention. Do not even observe it. Only pay attention to the *hwadu,* ignoring any thought. Make it your habit to dwell in this stage of mind, and then you will start feeling *the light* that dances and shines on the fundamental ground of all beings and all things. You will feel that spiritual bliss, which is absolutely beyond the ordinary sense of pleasure or happiness.

4.4. Into the dancing light

Of course, you can practice meditation not only after reading a literary text or watching a movie. Usually, the meaning of meditation suggests not doing so. However, literature and film can provide you with an ideal frame of mind to start your meditation with *kongans*. There is one more point I would like to make. Whether with or without literary reading, I would *not* recommend you spend a long time meditating. I would strongly suggest that after you spend some time meditating in this way, do not seek stillness more than is necessary. Instead, try to find composure while you work, talk to others, or carry on with other mundane everyday affairs.

Reading literature has the immense power to enable us to directly experience our free true nature, which I would compare to *the dancing light,* as the fundamental source of our thinking, only if we understand that literature is not to be judged according to a thematic value. A possible theme is a fake objective reality. There is no stable objective reality. All beings and objects arise and disappear in the sphere of Emptiness. To realize Emptiness or stillness in every facet of life is to become Emptiness as fullness, dancing and engendering all things and phenomena. Yet novels and films as artworks are special devices that place us in the midst of the whirlpool of Hamlet seeking revenge for his father's death or Ahab's overly strong desire to kill Moby Dick. Yet we finally reach stillness beyond this mad passion and the inhuman object.

In the depths of reality, stillness and peace are not opposed to movement. Stillness and peace are at the center of movement. In *Samadhi,* stillness is recognized to be identical to movement. In the *Heart Sutra,* Emptiness and form are identical. This is nonsensical to the ego, the separate, perceiving (with the power of self-importance) sense, because the ego itself is split, and thus it creates duality. To the thinking ego, everything is in a dual form. Literature and film offer us opportunities to transcend the subject's conceptual relation with the object, as implied in Descartes' famous statement, "I think, therefore I am." From Levinas' ethical perspective, the reader becomes passive toward the other, the exterior. The aesthetic way paved toward this dimension is the sublime.

In this light, your focus while reading a literary work or watching a movie that incites your imagination is close to the state of *Samadhi;* it is one of the closest ways to the experience of Emptiness as the Transmiddle Path without attachment to what seems to be an objective reality. In fact, the Buddha encourages questions and doubt, and he does so especially in the *Kalama Sutta.*[45] In this way, literature directly allows us to experience Emptiness, the genuine nature of ourselves, and the universe.

At the center of our being is the space for Emptiness, untouched by the duality formed by pleasure and pain, or happiness and suffering— Emptiness that gives rise to genuine wisdom. This little point of Emptiness that lies beyond the function of intellectuality and emotions can be revealed by religion. Sudden awakening in Ch'an/Seon/Zen Buddhism would expose the meditation practitioner to true spirituality and liberation from anxiety

---

[45] Larry Rosenberg, *Three Steps to Awakening: A Practice for Bringing Mindfulness to Life* (Boston: Shambhala, 2013), 15.

and suffering. This book explains that the primary purpose of the literary text in general, and Gothic fiction in particular, is to lead readers to this insight into such spiritual freedom that would make all the darkness and cruelty of life disappear.

In this way, the postmodern thought and insight of the thinkers discussed in the present study are very close to the knowledge and wisdom presented in Buddhist philosophy. Nowadays, East and West are being brought together to share different thoughts generated in different cultures more than ever before in human history. Yet rather than enjoying different ways of thinking, Western analytic philosophy secures the higher position. For all that, there have been constant influxes of Eastern cultures and religions into Western society, and Eastern thought has always unmistakably pointed to the dimension beyond analytic thought. Thinkers in this postmodern age especially cannot dismiss Eastern thought, which teaches us what a Western analytic mode of thinking wishes to attain more than ever before. The merging of the different ways of thinking will allow us to have a vivid vision of genuine humanity.

In both Eastern and Western thought in contemporary literature and film, with regard to postmodern ethics and Buddhism in particular, the ultimate reality of our lives and the whole universe is the dimension of genuinely transcendental, unrestrictive love. Only as we surrender our ego power to this non-dual love will we also be sufficiently wise to realize that God, the all-embracing truth, is our true self.

CHAPTER FIVE

GOTHIC FICTION IN MEDITATION:
DR. JEKYLL AND MR. HYDE
AND *THE PICTURE OF DORIAN GRAY*

5.1. The sublime effect of Gothic fiction in meditation

I would like to begin this chapter with some remarks to remind you about and to reinforce the most crucial points I have made throughout this book. First, the terms (pure) "consciousness" or "awareness" as employed by contemporary spiritual leaders mean more than what psychologists, psychoanalysts, or many philosophers indicate—the mental state of truly being awake, which takes up one tenth of the whole mind, while the rest of it is the unconscious. Consciousness, from the spiritual viewpoint, is the purest state of mind that lies beyond consciousness and the unconscious mind. It is beyond the reach of language, any expression, or even thought. You can encounter the true self or pure consciousness/awareness, live as it, and use it only as you realize the hard fact of the fleeting nature of every being and every thing in existence. This fleeting nature does not simply mean that "presence" is possible on the basis of nihilistic nothingness, worthlessness, vanity, or the futility of life. The essence of pure consciousness is infinity. Infinity indicates that your fundamental consciousness is not restricted to being your individual one.

The immaculate consciousness of you and all others are at a single point where there is no flow of time. As Jesus said, "Before Abraham, I *am*" (John 8:58). The Emptiness is one point and all universes. What is referred to as "the Holy Spirit" is always "now" and "here." In true reality, every being and every thing does not age in the flow of time; it is completed before it begins. All phenomena are different transient physical/mental/material forms of the one consciousness. As far as Jesus Christ is a name for the truth like Shakyamuni Buddha, he is right to say, "I am the way and the truth and the life. No one comes to the Father except through me" (John 14:6). As an embodiment of the absolute truth, Shakyamuni also represents limitless infinity. There is a famous story in Buddhism that, when breathing his last, Shakyamuni said that even though he taught for 49 years after his spiritual enlightenment, he had taught nothing. We all have the same consciousness that Jesus and Shakyamuni had. In Kantian terms, it is "subjective univocity." It is both individual and universal. In Buddhism, it is said that if a sentient being is unable to be enlightened to the reality that their self is the truth now and here, it will take eons for them to finally realize it.

Therefore, stopping our thinking and craving, and thus recovering our fundamental composure, is similar to searching for and finding what you forgot or lost in the remote past. Pure consciousness takes its form here and now, but it is prior to the form. That is why Levinas employs such words as "pre-originary." One of the artistic genres to perform such work is the Gothic one. There is no gate to the realm of truth you can be aware of because truth always takes phenomenal forms, and thus all phenomena can be gates to truth. However, a great Gothic work of art, through its power of shock and horror, can help you, the reader, destroy the shell of the ego.

From the historical perspective, postmodern ethics emerged after modernism, and in a different way to postmodernism *per se*. It is now the predominant trend in which critical theory is radically developing toward spirituality. The crucial issue of postmodern ethics is removing the shell of the ego, whose power of reasoning and feeling creates a self-centered illusory world. In the history of aesthetics and literary criticism, the thematic approach had been the classical, stereotypical view that lasted up until the end of modernism, when the seemingly right theme of the totality of the text was considered of utmost importance. Modernism is now much criticized for its tyranny of the Enlightenment, which necessarily needed rigid rules for governing a nation and for a totalizing theme in literary criticism.

Gothic horror, or Gothic fiction, is usually ignored and dismissed as a genre of a chaotic and grotesque nature. The Gothic genre seems to be thus compared to the classical one. That way of thought is a more pre-modernist or modernist way of thinking, which would be represented by the tyranny of empirical and authoritarian knowledge rather than the postmodernist mode of liberal thought's search for truth. Gothic fiction offers us opportunities to encounter the unaccepted, the exterior of the human individual and collective ego all at once with suspense and thrill. It has a strong power to enable us to break through and reach outside reason and emotion.

After the end of modernism, when there remained nostalgia for the Enlightenment in the new era of postmodernity, that is, of postmodernism *per se* and postmodern ethics, what became critical was not the subject or message, but how the literary text leads us to realize the true reality outside the illusory world of the egoic dream or, to put it simply, what lies outside language itself. The true reality, or the ultimate reality, is Emptiness without the dreamlike context constructed by the ego. Nonetheless, at the same time, the dream is the form (appearance or state) of the Emptiness that takes place in the given culture and era. Therefore, as in the *Heart Sutra*, "Emptiness is form, form is Emptiness."[46] Gothic fiction awakens us to this solid fact that even the ultimate reality and illusion are one and two, More exactly, they are *not one, not two*.

In the Mahayana Buddhist view, sudden enlightenment means an instant and remarkably strong realization of the purest, unconditioned reality beyond conceptions. Gothic fiction is distinctly characteristic of an immediate opening of the dimension of spirituality in the moment of the *postmodern sublime* (more spiritual sublime). Gothic masterpieces have truly struck enduring chords in the public mind.

While Vipassana meditation or mindfulness, prevalent in the Theravada Buddhist tradition and now also in the US, is more on the side of gradual enlightenment due to the observation style, Zen, especially keyword meditation in the Mahayana tradition, emphasizes sudden awakening. Both Vipassana and Zen have merits of their own, and also share a great deal of the same nature. We examined how we read a literary masterpiece like *Hamlet* in the last chapter in both Vipassana and Zen styles. In this chapter, I would like to apply my synthetic idea to Gothic masterpieces.

I would like to show you how the aesthetic experience of the *sublime* is produced effectively by the *affective* mood of two Gothic novels. Gothic fiction engenders excessive fear, a lack of security, thrill, and suspense in the reader. The excess of the eerie and mysterious Gothic mood freezes you. It stops your thinking, and that suspension of the flow of thinking has the effect of causing the *meditative* frame of mind to encounter the innermost nature. When your thinking has stopped, you experience an *immediate awakening* with weak intensity. Thus, Gothic fiction is like a vast *kongan,* whose role it is to take the reader beyond itself. It shows the *deadlock* of logical thinking and language, and *hwadus* serve as a gate to the dimension of spirituality.

To briefly elaborate, following my discussion in Chapter Three, *kongans* and *hwadus* are anecdotes and keywords that lead the Ch'an/Seon/Zen meditator beyond language and thought into Emptiness, their truly unlimited self, or the ultimate reality of life and the universe. Literature and film should be a specially provided ground for the reader and viewer to break the finite, small, prison-like world of the separate, individual world and enter the cosmos of the whole, *dharmakaya,* or the Buddha body in

---

[46] Thich Nhat Hanh, *Awakening of the Heart: Essential Buddhist Sutras and Commentaries* (Berkeley: Parallax Press, 2012), 420.

Buddhist terms.[47] The reader or viewer would acquire a keen comprehension of Emptiness, where every being and every thing is equal in terms of dependent co-origination without fundamental superiority or inferiority.[48]

To continue with this point on literature and art, in exploring how Gothic novels can bring a moment of sudden awakening (as in Ch'an/Seon/Zen Buddhism) to the reader, it is necessary that we first examine Edmund Burke's and Immanuel Kant's thoughts on Gothic fiction and the Gothic sublime. "The Gothic sublime" here indicates the effects of *the delicate sublime sensibility or sensitivity that the reader or the viewer has while immersed in the grotesque mood, suspense, thrill, and loss of security of the Gothic genre.* The pivotal issue is that the impact of terror and horror gives rise to the sublime because the mind has "a power surpassing any standard of sense" of finite nature.[49] As the reader, you become absorbed in the horrific and grotesque mood. You experience the excess of that mood. You transcend reason and emotion.

I discussed the two supreme Gothic novels, well-known to many and the most continually cinematized (Mary Shelley's *Frankenstein* and Bram Stoker's *Dracula*), in my previous book. The examples I take here are *The Strange Case of Dr. Jekyll and Mr. Hyde* (1886) by Robert Louis Stevenson and Oscar Wilde's *The Picture of Dorian Gray* (1890). I will demonstrate how the reader can read the two most widely discussed *fin de siècle* (the Decadent movement in Western literature at the end of the 19th century) Gothic novels. These two texts have less of an effect in terms of fear and shock compared to *Frankenstein* (1818) and *Dracula* (1897). Yet these texts break the dual structure of the reader's ego construct and offer the reader an opportunity to glimpse the genuine reality of humanity.

Although, as a reader or viewer, you experience fear, horror, abhorrence, and shock, you may not realize what you have experienced. What do I mean? However frightened you are by the horrible scene, the story is not the life story of yourself. The story is someone else's. Then you, as a spectator or observer, accept the conventional thematic approach with moral themes that you have heard from others or learned at school. The set moral ideas overwhelm the reader's experience, and hence the reader ignores what lies beyond the moral issues. In most cases, a literary text does not yield such an immediate and dramatic effect on the reader. In interpreting the artwork with the theme given from outside, you would likely feel intellectually and emotionally distanced from the story and would not involve the sublime, which would carry you to the spiritual dimension.

---

[47] Lee, *Postmodern Ethics*, 16, 172.

[48] Humphries, *Reading Emptiness*, 32.

[49] Kant, *Critique of Judgment*, 106.

Here lies a new task for the critic. Today, it is usually a professor's obligation to write serious papers on literary texts or films. Critics, however, do not have to approach it in those terms. The case could be similar to introducing a book or film to audiences or, more simply, to friends by writing a short review. A short review of a book or film almost always appears to be no more than a very brief synopsis of the story. I sincerely hope that this book will create a positive turn to help all cases of talking about or discussing a literary work or film. I believe that not only a serious paper and review but a simple brief synopsis can convey a slice of the spiritual nature of the given work; a review of a Gothic work would especially need such a style of writing.

To begin with, criticism has to elucidate the reader's transformation—to intellectually explain the reader's spiritual experience. There is a common saying that states if you read literature, you will learn to know yourself better. Yet knowing yourself is not as simple as that. To know yourself better does not mean obtaining more knowledge of what you are really fond of and what you have a distaste for. To know your personality better would bring you a phenomenal change so that you can think you are now "a new person"—one who is better qualified to see how you think and act clearly in the world. It is a transformation of A into B that takes place on the level of mentality and behavior.

In discussing what happens to you, the reader, while reading a literary text, I do not mean to talk about this simple thematic change or more learning taking place. Rather, I mean to discuss a process by which the reader's ego power is decreased. Reading fiction has the power to transmute you, just as meditation practice transmutes a practitioner. The eventual goal of both reading literature/watching films and practicing meditation/silent prayer is the "abolition of the ego" and attaining spiritual awakening.

As you are immersed in the horrific, mysterious, and grotesque mood that stops your thinking, you also experience "a power surpassing any standard" of ordinary feelings. That extraordinary power *transcends sensation and conceptual understanding*. What I call Gothic excess lies beyond language expression for any theme. As I have discussed in the previous chapters, in Mahayana Buddhism, *sudden awakening* is the powerful result of meditation practice. One attains an awakening instantaneously, not in a general process. The transcendental nature of Gothic excess breaks the shell of the thinking ego. Even though you are not aware of it, the opening to the exterior is being formed. Of course, I do not mean all Gothic works have this power. The great Gothic stories I introduce here, as well as those I discussed in my previous book, have this power of breaking through.

In order to make clear the certainty and validity of what I maintain, I would first like to turn to Edmund Burke's 1757 treatise *A Philosophical Enquiry into the Origin of Our Ideas of the Sublime and Beautiful*, where he elaborates on fear as the source of the sublime. Not pleasure but pain, conflict, suffering, insecurity, and terror are greater sources of the aesthetic sublime. Terror is "the ruling principle of the sublime."[50] Beyond question, this tragic ending is not for us simply to enjoy in the ordinary sense; it broadens our mind by tearing down its limitations.

I would also like to point out that Kant even goes on to say that the sublime is "the name given to what is absolutely large" or "great" and that it is found in a "formless" object: what is actually presented to us is not precisely the formless object itself but rather our own imagination "in all its boundlessness."[51] Kant's idea of the sublime was even developed into the postmodern sublime by contemporary thinkers such as Jean-Luc Nancy. For the sake of convenience, I will come back to the postmodern sublime later when I discuss specific Gothic novels.

Both Burke and Kant commonly acknowledge the capacity of the sublime experience that leads us beyond ordinary senses and experience. This experience of sublimity is not just to be understood merely as an aesthetic experience. The deep aesthetic experience of going beyond the finite is a different form of religious experience in terms of the outward identities. Whether it is called aesthetic or religious, the profound experience of Emptiness, or the true self, gives you the chance to go through the feeling that transcends ordinary feelings that arise from the five senses. As the boundary of the sense perception and the ego is broken, your real self reveals itself to you. However, the real self is not your individual self like your ego. It reveals itself with the medium of filtering with the specific values of period and culture. The "beauty" of art is what reveals the exterior of the restricted and conceptual values trapped in a specific time and space. That is to say, the true self is the light that always moves—*dances*—from beyond into time and space.

5.2. *The Strange Case of Dr. Jekyll and Mr. Hyde*: Novel, movie, musical

I propose that, in English literature, the most "graphic" Gothic story that effectively reveals the vanity of the binary opposition of the ego is *The*

---

[50] Edmund Burke, *A Philosophical Enquiry into the Origin of our Ideas of the Sublime and Beautiful* (Oxford: Oxford University Press, 1990), 54.
[51] Kant, *Critique of Judgment*, 114.

Strange Case of Dr. Jekyll and Mr. Hyde by Robert Louis Stevenson (1886). It is one of the two best *fin de siècle* novels along with Oscar Wilde's *The Picture of Dorian Gray* (1890). *Fin de siècle* is the name for (or characteristic of) novels of the Decadence movement of the end of the 19ᵗʰ century. Published only four years apart, both have great power to lead us to the ultimate reality of the self and the world through an atmosphere of mystery and the supernatural. The novella *Dr. Jekyll and Mr. Hyde* shows Dr. Henry Jekyll's failure to liberate himself from the prison-like realm of his ego. The special power of the novella that attracts the reader arises from the clear comparisons and contrasts between the two opposite sides of the binary ego construct.

The events that take place in this novella are frightening and shocking. The story consists of murders and other kinds of violence and unsolved mysteries that we could only possibly commit if we threw out our moral nature and self-restraint. I will not repeat the trite moral explanation of the story that is so well-known to the public. Instead, I would like to start by explaining my point regarding the novella as a work of *art*. While reading the story and experiencing its mood, we have the opportunity to experience a pre-reflective aesthetic force that overflows the unexpected feelings of terror, violently opening our mind toward their unadulterated, inconceivable self. Although texts in all literary genres often provide us with the same effect, "Gothic fiction has the most notable features and power to bend our mind to the exteriority."[52]

The unique feature of this text is that the horrible Mr. Edward Hyde and the good-natured Dr. Henry Jekyll are two opposite halves of the same person. All that Hyde does is what Jekyll cannot do as a well-acknowledged and respected doctor in London society. Hyde is none other than the appalling beast-like being in Dr. Jekyll that is always seeking a chance to be unfettered. The novella opens with the news that Hyde beat a girl with a stick and even stepped over her body as it lay on the street. This news has the effect of appalling you, the reader, right at the outset. You would take a stance to look at the whole story from the exterior of the mundane life that we live with the egoic power of cognizance and understanding, and then begin to encounter what is coming from beyond.

As he drinks the potion, Jekyll, a decent doctor, changes into the murderous Hyde and commits crimes that he would never do in his normal mental state. When he drinks the potion for the first time, Jekyll feels

---

[52] Lee, *Postmodern Ethics*, 99.

"younger, lighter, happier in body."[53] At the same time, he also experiences "a heady recklessness, a current of disordered sensual images running like a millrace in [his] fancy."[54] As is revealed in the last chapter of the novella, "Henry Jekyll's Full Statement of the Case," Jekyll "was driven to reflect deeply and inveterately on that hard law of life, which lies at the root of religion and is one of the most plentiful springs of distress."[55]

After his scientific investigation is done successfully, he continues in pursuit of freeing the moral side of the nature of his life which "has advanced infallibly in one direction."[56] The freedom he wanted was also his nature, but he had repressed that animal nature in him. The potion makes Jekyll feel free. In fact, he was aware of his "profound duplicity,"[57] which is the profoundly dual nature of the ego. With his murderous impulses, Hyde would do anything that the moralistic Jekyll would not do.

> I, for my part, from the nature of my life, advanced infallibly in one direction and in one direction only. It was on the moral side, and in my own person, that I learned to recognize the thorough and primitive duality of man; I saw that, of the two natures that contended in the field of my consciousness, even if I could rightly be said to be either, it was only because I was radically both; and from an early date, even before the course of my scientific discoveries had begun to suggest the most naked possibility of such a miracle, I had learned to dwell with pleasure, as a beloved day-dream, on the thought of the separation of these elements. If each, I told myself, could but be housed in separate identities, life would be relieved of all that was unbearable; the unjust delivered from the aspirations might go his way, and remorse of his more upright twin; and the just could walk steadfastly and securely on his upward path, doing the good things in which he found his pleasure, and no longer exposed to disgrace and penitence by the hands of this extraneous evil. It was the curse of mankind that these incongruous fagots were thus bound together that in the agonized womb of consciousness, these polar twins should be continuously struggling. How, then, were they dissociated?[58]

Jekyll is first delighted with transforming into Hyde and rejoices in the freedom the monstrous creature has. Yet, as he finds he cannot stop turning into Hyde voluntarily, he decides to get rid of him by taking his own life.

---

[53] Robert Louis Stevenson, *Strange Case of Dr Jekyll and Mr Hyde and Other Tales* (Oxford World's Classics). Edited by Roger Luckhurst. (Oxford: Oxford University Press, 2008), 54.
[54] Ibid., 54.
[55] Ibid., 52.
[56] Ibid., 53.
[57] Ibid., 52.
[58] Ibid., 53.

This means that by excluding both the good and evil sides of one person, the novella leads us to glimpse the ultimate reality, or the state of emptiness of the good and evil that lies beyond the illusory nature of our judgment. All other elements together create horror and dread. The foggy, sinister, and uncanny background of the city is also a setting of the Gothic fiction genre.

The novella is also framed from the viewpoint of bystanders and a detective who intensify the puzzle together. The final event of the novella involves Dr. Jekyll finally committing suicide just when others, Utterson (a prominent London lawyer) and Poole (his butler), break down the door of his laboratory. Jekyll makes a serious attempt to cast off the other side of his social identity, Hyde, who was his companion for a while. This reveals the self-destructive nature of our ego. The novella does not show that the polar opposites of the personality of one (Jekyll and Hyde) supplements the other so that readers may enjoy a happy ending. The gap between the two magnifies as Jekyll calls Hyde an extremely selfish creature. [59] The opposites—Jekyll and Hyde—do not show any solid, tangible result from Jekyll's struggle with Hyde. What remains at the end is literally nothing.

Nevertheless, the novella exerts the power of our (the readers') sublime experience precisely because of this tragic ending. What really takes place is not the simple state of "no-thing" but "emptiness," which gives birth to your experience of the sublime. We experience the sublime as the opposites conflict with each other and excessively struggle. You, as the reader, cannot fully accept the experience of the sublime as you try to understand the story with a theme and attach it to some explainable point. Happy endings do not make us happy. You would experience the deep feeling of the sublime as the suffering heightens and reaches the tragic ending. As you go through this process, you come to lessen the power of the ego, and your mind grows to accept all phenomena and all possible thoughts. [60]

There have been many stage and cinematized versions of *Dr. Jekyll and Mr. Hyde* in different countries all over the world. I would like to comment on *Jekyll & Hyde: Direct from Broadway,* a 2001 TV film of the Broadway production captured live in performance, and the 2003 TV movie *Dr. Jekyll and Mr. Hyde* produced by Universal Pictures in the U.K. The movie begins with a coach riding along the narrow roads of the city of London at night. It stops before Jekyll's house and two people get out—Poole, Jekyll's chief butler, and Gabriel John Utterson, Jekyll's friend. You might agree that the name "Utterson" fits his profession, a lawyer, and that as such he sounds like a very conventional person, a son of traditional society. It may be the case in that sense that he is a most commonsensical person. Utterson is the

---

[59] Ibid., 72.
[60] See Lee, *Postmodern Ethics*, Chap. 6 on *Dracula* and Chap. 7 on *Frankenstein*.

narrator of the novel and the one whose reading of Jekyll's letter to him forms the whole film.

The fact that the film starts with the scene to which we come back at the end has the effect of keeping the viewers within the story's scope without extending its timeframe. Utterson and Poole run into Jekyll's room, where he is dying after drinking poison to kill Hyde. They arrive just after Jekyll has killed himself. It is similar to, yet more effective than, the technique of flashback, where an interpolated scene takes the story back in time from the present point. This link of the first and the last scenes lets us know that the ultimate truth we need to realize lies nowhere else than in the here and now. In the film, it seems that the theological issue of creation playing God and good and evil are enlarged. Jekyll rejects the existence of God in the film. The film tries to touch the sense of such common but sensitive matters of the public. Those issues are dealt with in Mary Shelley's *Frankenstein*. The film lays weight on those issues that were important not only to Victorian society but to a large number of contemporary audiences.

The hypocrisy of Victorian society is also handled importantly in the story of Jekyll and Hyde. Sir Danvers Carew is a member of Parliament, who is a supreme symbol of the hypocritical upper class. He does not appear in the original novella, but the movie and the musical both place him as a victim of Hyde. Hyde brutally beats Carew to death with a stick that was handed down to him from his father. Carew is killed as a member of the upper class in a hypocritical society. In the movie, Carew shows his generosity by taking Mabel to Jekyll's house to ask him to take her as his servant, but it later turns out to be hypocrisy. He used to go to different secret places for erotic pleasure, and Mabel is a daughter from his relationship with a prostitute Carew used to visit. Mabel is Carew's daughter, just like his Sarah (Emma in the musical), who is a daughter of his born in wedlock.

In both the film and the musical, there are two women who represent the upper class and the lower class. In the film, the upper-class woman (whom he comes to marry at the end of the musical) is Sarah Carew. In the film, Hyde rapes her not only in the street but even when she is very sick in bed as a result. The lower-class woman is Mabel in the film and Lucy in the musical, and Lucy is herself a prostitute in the musical, while her mother is not a character in the musical. Jekyll's relationships with the two women would arouse the viewers' sympathy for Jekyll or enmity for Hyde, just as Dracula's relationship with Mina in Francis Ford Coppola's film does. Ned, the boy who serves Jekyll by bringing chemicals to him, is also added in the film as one who irritates and is to be killed by Hyde. In the novella and the musical, Poole helps Jekyll by finding and bringing these chemicals to him.

In both the musical and the film, the transformation scene must have a great effect on the audience. In Stevenson's novella, Jekyll goes through a metamorphosis into Hyde before Lanyon, a good, sober-minded doctor and his friend, in order to prove his denunciation is wrong. In the film and the musical, as might be expected, the metamorphosis is done for the audience and, as might be expected, the appearance of Hyde is not remarkably horrible, as the novella works on the reader's imagination without using visual images. In the novella, he changes into his evil, conscience-free side of being with a misshapen, younger body. In the last scene of the musical, even bringing about Emma's and the audience's sympathy is possible.

For both the film and theoretical adaptations, mise-en-scène is very important in two specific senses. First, because Jekyll's experiments take place in a secret room, the laboratory is placed at the core of both the film and the musical very successfully. I would especially like to mention the mise-en-scène in which Jekyll destroys his laboratory in the movie. He first frees the experimental birds from their cage and throws the cage at his experimental tools and breaks them. Of course, this means that he is firmly resolute in stopping Hyde from returning. He is determined to set himself free from the darkness and miserableness of the cruelty. However, we must notice that he does *not* free the birds so that they may really become free. As it turns out in Utterson's reading of Jekyll's letter to him, Jekyll frees himself from his bondage to Hyde by killing himself. It rather means that Jekyll becomes free to kill Hyde by committing suicide. He burns his papers for the experiment, yet *only in his room!* This symbolizes that he is not really free from Hyde and could not be so, no matter how determined he is. This corresponds to the scene in the musical where Jekyll condemns Hyde in the confrontation scene. Also, the hallucination scenes in which he kills Mabel leave a strong impression on the viewers with a great mise-en-scène effect. The breaking of the mirror means that Jekyll has now lost his last conscience power to see Hyde. Now Hyde is not only his image reflected in the mirror but has also become Jekyll. Hyde kills Mabel by slitting her throat, and the two opposite sides, Jekyll and Hyde, then kill themselves.

In the final analysis, what the novella, the film, and the musical make the audience feel is not too much either of the good or the evil side in their conventional definitions! The good-evil moral issue or the creation theme are small matters. The story of Jekyll and Hyde is really about liberating humanity from its small prison. This is not possible by identifying what is good and what is evil. Each of the good and evil sides are not really to be defined so. It is possible only as we realize the ultimate reality that the human-created moral concepts of good and evil are just supplementary to each other. Jekyll and Hyde deconstruct the concepts and lay bare the necessity of supplementation to us. The awakened spiritual person would think and behave in the ultimate reality of the Transmiddle movement of embracing both good and evil, not becoming either. The human mind can acknowledge all beings and things only as it sees its reflection in others. At any rate, the novella struck an enduring chord with the public.

I recommend you spend some time meditating on the novella as a *kongan*. In the light of Ch'an/Seon/Zen Buddhism, the story as a *kongan* reveals to us the dilemma of the judgment between good and evil, dignity and inhuman cruelty. At the end of the novella, neither Jekyll nor Hyde defeats the other. In simple fact, Jekyll is Hyde and Hyde is Jekyll! The relationship between Jekyll and Hyde is more of oneness than the relation between Hamlet and Claudius, since Jekyll and Hyde are the two different natures of one person. The ultimate reality is never revealed within the network of judgments based upon dualism that brings a hierarchical structure. Jekyll finds no hope of living in peace, and he kills himself as a whole in killing Hyde. Jekyll's killing of Hyde means that the ego intensity can never reveal its source. The ego can only produce the result of the judgment that depends on relative comparisons and contrasts. After finishing this long *kongan,* you can begin some sitting or walking meditation with the *hwadu* from this *kongan.*

The *hwadu* would be "Why does Jekyll commit suicide?" or "What does Jekyll desire in committing suicide?" More abstractly, it could also be "What is beyond good and evil? or "What lies beyond our intellectual, rational judgment?" All such concise questions would share the same goal of stopping your thinking and enabling you to go beyond finitude, as the most well-known *hwadus* "What is this?" and "What am I?" do. "This" or "I" is the transcendental but also immanent *ultimate reality.* Of course, I do not mean that you will necessarily be able to tell what infinity is. Infinity can never be conveyed in any kind of description. Yet you would have the sensibility of what you do not know. As your experiences of the Gothic sublime accumulate, that sensibility of the "don't-know mind" will give you the wisdom to feel the ultimate reality, which lies beyond the binary opposition of thinking.

As I said in the discussion of *Hamlet* in Chapter Four, "Good and evil personalities are just conditioned phenomena." The novella as a *kongan* asks the reader how we can escape the fundamental human problem of dualism. This dual nature should not have to be simply considered as good and evil in a strictly conservative, Victorian, Christian sense. Jekyll and Victorian society cannot be identified as the absolute good. Good nature cannot really be good without embracing the other side that is considered as evil. Jekyll is a spiritually inquisitive person and inquires about the dual nature of humanity. Cruel nature is "natural," although it is the "lower" part of the soul, as Jekyll says in the last chapter. He decides to release the side of himself and all others that are inclined to experiencing pleasure. He reasons that he would be able to eradicate the violent, darker side of himself and all humans that make all unbearable after he first separates the two. He wrongly thinks that a dual nature is a curse upon humans. Like Victor Frankenstein in Mary Shelley's *Frankenstein* who creates a human (monster), he enters the realm of the unknown and unknowable.

As you practice meditation after reading the whole novella, you will let go of the dualistic misconception of good and evil that has brought on your mood of anxiety and become calm. The true self surely can be called no-self or non-self. I have discussed the real self as the power that breaks down the boundary between the ego and its object. This real self or the sublime cannot be explained in language, which is formed by the ego. Because it is non-self, as the first sentence of the *Tao-te Ching*, written by Laozi nearly 2,600 years ago, teaches us, Tao that can be described in language is not the real Tao. Tao, God, or the real self is the exteriority of the ego—before, beyond, or beneath the realm of all perceptions and concepts. It is the universal relating in itself, and awaking from the illusory form of being attached to thinking and the conceptualization of the ego as dreaming is the goal of religions, philosophy, literature, and the arts.

Good and evil are defined just as how they are seen in a particular situation. For example, "Thou shalt not kill" would not be a good maxim in a situation where one is to kill an enemy or be killed. The real issue is not any kind of conceptualization of good and evil. Exclusively the duality of humanity is more than "natural." The mirror of the mind makes both concepts. As far as I am concerned, I was surely shocked at what happens in the novel (and the films and musicals). Stevenson's novella deconstructs the duality of human nature and leads us beyond it. In fact, all Western works of literature and art manifest it. Philosophers, both of East and West, still talk about it, yet do not adopt Shakyamuni's enlightenment to their heart. If they did, they would really be open to the most profound depth of humanity.

After all, the ultimate reality beyond the opposite poles—good and evil, being and non-being, presence and absence—is your fundamental, purest mind beyond egoic judgment that separates you from itself (and thus from others). It occupies the Transmiddle position that both embraces and transcends the opposites. The Transmiddle, or simply transcendence, as such alone is the most profound dimension of all animate and inanimate existences in oneness. It lives over time and space, and thus you cannot think of any experience from the past or present or plan what you will do in the future. It is beyond the limitations of physical existence and mental function and thus is independent of them. There is only full awareness of that dimension of perfectly uncontaminated impeccable purity. You can think and act on the basis of this dimension of truth where everything actually takes form. There is no knowing if Stevenson experienced this dimension, yet it is clear to me that he somehow reached a deep conviction that, in the deep reality of the true self, good and evil are truly one. It is your true self, and it is the true self of each and every one of us that lies beyond the material presence of all beings, things, and phenomena.

Our true self embraces and transcends presence, being, or good, which is only one side of the whole. Our spirituality is infinite. This is why Buddhists say that we as Buddhas are beyond life and death. Shakyamuni Buddha was awakened to the truth that he (his true self) was not really born, and thus would not die. To put it in other words, the true self is empty of any phenomena. It is Emptiness that produces the presence of phenomena. As mentioned in the previous chapter, this unlimited self is "subjective univocity" in Kantian terms.

If you realize that the ultimate reality is Emptiness, you welcome undisturbed feelings of stillness and bliss. It is the feeling of the sublime or *jouissance* you have after reading this Gothic work. In a blissful and unlimited state of mind, you transcend the level of egoic feelings such as anger, jealousy, anxiety, love as the feeling of being attached to an outside object, and hate. In the Deleuzean sense, you experience *becoming pure and imperceptible.*

In this way, *The Strange Case of Dr. Jekyll and Mr. Hyde* offers us a supreme and graphic example of the deconstruction of egoic feelings. By reading the novella or viewing a film or musical and by meditating on the *kongan* as mentioned earlier, you may glimpse the ultimate reality and grow spiritually. In view of reader-response criticism, the "implied" reader (Wolfgang Iser's notion) would be the one who accepts the Gothic sublimity of this novella. Such a reader is also the one who tends to deconstruct dualism and go beyond totality with ease. As you read the novella or watch the film in this light and experience the sublime, or *Samadhi* in the Buddhist sense, you will glimpse the dimension of non-duality, where you and the novella/movie are "not one, but not two"—phenomenally two, yet one in essence. We, the readers, enter into this wondrous movement of Emptiness that goes from non-phenomenal oneness to phenomenal duality and then back to non-phenomenal oneness. I call this creative movement the *dancing* of the light of truth.

5.3. *The Picture of Dorian Gray*: Novel and movie

Oscar Wilde's *The Picture of Dorian Gray* is another powerful example that offers us an opportunity to glimpse the exterior of the ego through the great Gothic sublime. First published in 1890, this novel shows us the prototype of the human ego that does not control but simply lets go of its sensuous desire.

In particular, Dorian Gray's story is outside the conventional, simple moral theme that is related to the concept of the flow of time. The matter of the destruction of the vain illusion of self-identity should be laid at the center here as well. Dorian's life story emphasizes the ego construct's illusion. The novel discloses Dorian's illusory identity to you, the reader, so that you may go beyond that illusion. However, it is very important to notice that you cannot transcend it with a poetic justice theme, according to which the work has been judged before.

The language of the Gothic sublime is "a mirror to infinity" in Michel Foucault's (1926-84) terms. [61] Reading this novel through a Gothic-postmodern lens will reveal that it is truly superb in that it points to the exteriority of the binary opposition formed by polar opposites of the ego's judgment—beauty and ugliness, future and past, positive and negative versions of self-identity, etc.

I would first like to present the plot of *Dorian Gray,* trying to integrate it with my thoughts on the similarity between meditation and literary reading. Above all, the novel is full of Gothic mood. The atmosphere of industrializing London is grotesque. The city is a place of immoral experiences of pleasure, crime, and irrational hedonism that includes sexual deviance, abuse of narcotics, blackmail, and murder. Dorian becomes a vindicator for these surroundings. All these examples—morality and immorality, the innocence of Dorian and his corruption, and real Dorian and the picture—illustrate binary, polar opposites.

He first becomes fascinated with Lord Henry Wotton's hedonism and indulges in sensuous pleasure. Realizing and panicking at the fact he is aging and that his beauty will fade, Dorian wishes to remain as young as he is portrayed in the picture painted by Basil Hallward (who is later killed by the narcissistic Dorian in a moment of egoic frenzy) and for his appearance in the painting to age instead:

---

[61] Michel Foucault, "Language to Infinity," in *Language, Counter-memory, Practice: Selected Essays and Interviews by Michel Foucault*, ed. Donald F. Bouchard (Ithaca: Cornell University Press, 1977), 23.

How sad it is! I shall grow old, and horrible, and dreadful. But this picture will remain always young. It will never be older than this particular day of June.... If it were only the other way! If it were I who was to be always young, and the picture that was to grow old! For that—for that—I would give everything! Yes, there is nothing in the whole world I would not give! I would give my soul for that![62]

Then Dorian indulges in pleasure, living a libertine life of amoral experiences, as he indeed stays young and the image in the picture ages with the horrible appearance that records the sins he commits. His pursuit of sensuous pleasure is directly tied to his own life. Dorian, as a handsome young man, becomes strongly attached to sensuous life right away. Living such a life eventually leads to his death. Toward the end of the story, Dorian decides that he will live a righteous life. But when he finds that there is only an even more hideous image of himself, Dorian goes on to destroy the picture, the only piece of evidence that proves his crimes: "The thing was still loathsome—more loathsome, if possible, than before—and the scarlet dew that spotted the hand seemed brighter, and more like blood newly spilled."[63] He takes a knife and stabs the picture, just as he had killed Basil Hallward with the same knife. In the last scene, he destroys himself as every evil deed done in the past comes full circle:

He looked round, and saw the knife that had stabbed Basil Hallward. He had cleaned it many times, till there was no stain left upon it. It was bright, and glistened. As it had killed the painter, so it would kill the painter's work, and all that that meant. It would kill the past, and when that was dead he would be free. ... He seized the thing, and stabbed the picture with it. There was a cry heard, and a crash. The cry was so horrible in its agony that the frightened servants woke, and crept out of their rooms.[64]

Then the servants of the household, on entering the locked attic, find Dorian lying in the form of the disfigured corpse and the picture with the original beauty of Dorian.[65] Dorian's violence of stabbing the picture only results in his death. This shocking last scene offers the reader a moment of the Gothic sublime, which unexpectedly leads you to face the exterior of the perceived knowledge and thinking process. What really matters is not the moral law. While the language goes on only to describe that evil deeds are limited to

---

[62] Oscar Wilde, *The Picture of Dorian Gray*, ed. Norman Page (Peterborough: Broadview Press Ltd., 1998), 65.
[63] Ibid., 249.
[64] Ibid., 250
[65] Ibid.

their circuit and do not reach outside, the scene as a whole short-circuits your brain.

I would not interpret this novel with a moral theme as so many conventional readers and critics have done up to now. Our task for ourselves and others is, by reading the novel or watching the film adaptation, to obtain pure consciousness with true wisdom. It can seem ironic that pure consciousness, the fountain of true wisdom, comes to us only when we stop taking pride in our thinking ability. Consciousness and its wisdom indicate the state of perfect wakefulness without a judgment by the ego, and it is how Ch'an/Seon/Zen works. In contrast to the horror scene, in this mental state of inner peace and stillness, you think and act without being attached to the outward form/appearance of the state of objects and phenomena that arises in the given time and space. It is the way of practicing love beyond empirical concepts of love and hatred, the absolute good beyond the concepts of good and evil.

The 2009 British fantasy-horror movie adaptation has a slightly different plot. It has Dorian's love story with Emily, the daughter of Lord Henry, who led Dorian to pleasure and corruption. (The film or musical adaptations of *Dracula* and *Dr. Jekyll and Mr. Hyde* also have such love stories.) Through his love story with Emily, the audience certainly comes to have sympathy for Dorian. Emily finds Dorian's pure heart beneath his life of pleasure and corruption, as all people know. Dorian recovers his innocent love, which he once felt for Sibyl Vane long ago, even Emily was born. He even repents his monstrous pursuit of pleasure. As he tries to confess to a Catholic priest, he wants to be "free." Just like Jekyll, he is unable to really let go of his life until the last moment.

Yet unlike the end of the original, and unlike Jekyll, it was Lord Henry through whom he comes to stab the horrible looking portrait of him and dies as a result. Dorian attempts to kill Henry, as he did Basil who painted it. On seeing the hideousness of the picture of Dorian, Henry throws a lit lamp at the portrait. As the painting burns, Henry escapes from the attic and locks the door. Emily demands Dorian give her the key, yet Dorian goes on to kill the figure in the picture, and thus himself, as Henry pulls Emily out. She leaves her father, Henry, and she remains in the dark about the secret of Dorian's youth. In the end, not only Dorian Gray but also the readers face silence, just as Hamlet and the readers of his story do at the end with his death. Apathy or indifference is the last phase of the whole emotional flux and the sublime momentum to break through the door to the spiritual.

I know many would still try to interpret *The Picture of Dorian Gray* with the old theme of good and evil, but first and foremost, the issue of the *duality* of the human ego and the way of *deconstructing* it so that the readers and viewers can experience the sublime and glimpse the *exterior* is the genuinely wise way of handling the work. It is even the *irony* of the false self that the Gothic mood leads us to. It is at the end of this work of art that we find peace and stillness. As we have seen, sages and thinkers of the past and many contemporary people share this thought of the Gothic sublime! The plot of *Dorian Gray* is set in the *dichotomy* formed by his own beauty and his hideous image in the picture due to his aging and egoic mentality, the result of which is his death in the end. Precisely because he is innocent and pure, he quickly deteriorates. Toward the end, before he dies, Dorian regrets his past deeds and decides that he will live a new life. Yet he turns against the picture and stabs it. His ego cannot accept his conscience. His death is actually in the nature of a suicide like Jekyll's. His innocent and pure mind is only part of his ego, and his adulterated mind is another aspect of the ego. Dorian's story shows us that between his innocence and his corruption, he fails to accept things, especially *dukkha*, or insufficiency/unsatisfactoriness, that is, aging, as they are. The novel ends with the extinction of both Dorian's hedonic pleasure and his ego that pursued it. In reality, his hedonic pleasure has accumulated affliction. Although he was agitated by the picture that shows his gradual aging and worsening nature, Dorian just ignored it.

If you live a mundane life, trying to remain in the Vipassana style just to observe whatever is happening to you and around you, you would realize that pain and pleasure are two different sides of one nature. You can read the novel using Vipassana/mindfulness meditation. Then you will know that what destroys Dorian is his ego, his individual self that does not accept *dukkha* as the equal counterpart of the whole of life. He only chooses one side—pleasure, youth, and beauty. Such Vipassana/mindfulness meditation has a special effect of calming one's anxious and split mind and putting it in a middle state so that you can realize the impermanence of mental and physical conditions. They all arise and pass away. The purpose of the phrase "What is this?" is to lead you outside the circuit of the ego.

This kind of reading is not of a traditional and conventional style. We try to combine those two methods of meditation to explore and explain how the reader/viewer's mind may confront the other, or the real self that always transcends (without any signified meaning) the literary language itself and comes to glimpse the ultimate reality, that is, the innermost and real self of the reader/viewer themselves. The ego is unable to recognize the solid reality of the whole—pain and pleasure, happiness and unhappiness, beauty and ugliness, good and evil are actually the different appearances of one whole. The Transmiddle Zone, as the whole, is out of the reach of the ego's folly.

The middle path in *The Picture of Dorian Gray* is the *no value judgment zone* between the handsomeness of Dorian and the decaying nature and hideous look of his picture. The end of the story, like that of *Dr. Jekyll and Mr. Hyde,* shows you the vision of the debacle of the whole of Dorian's ego construct. The conclusion leaves nothing—possible themes or personas— to which you would cling. In other words, the truly other side of the egoic nature is not to be described in language or even perceived. The Transmiddle Path is approachable only through the deconstruction of the ontological relations of pleasure and pain, good and evil, old and new, beauty and ugliness, past and future, and presence and absence. The language and thought of the ego cannot reach the Transmiddle Zone.

Again, my discussion directly employs Buddhist thought on Emptiness, infinity, *kongan,* and *hwadu,* as well as the postmodern philosophy of contemporary Western thinkers. A *hwadu* for solving the riddle of the enigma in *Dorian Gray* would be, "Where do the opposite aspects of Dorian lead us?" By meditating with this *hwadu,* we would glimpse the dimension of Emptiness, the boundless radiance of limitless consciousness. To consider literary reading from this perspective on the fundamental aim of literary texts is to lead the reader to glimpse this deepest reality through the experience of the sublime. Although the forms of literary reading and meditation seem to be different, the two have the same goal—to reach the ultimate reality beyond language and thought. As Jean-François Lyotard and Jean-Luc Nancy emphatically and repeatedly say in their essays in *Of the Sublime,* a collection on Kant's explanation of the sublime, the sublime feeling is *a spiritual feeling of liberation* that detaches you from your sensory perception.

Both *fin de siècle* novels, *Dr. Jekyll and Mr. Hyde* and *Dorian Gray,* deal with the binary opposition of the self with the concept of the supernatural identity of the double or *doppelgänger. Dr. Jekyll and Mr. Hyde* is rather short and simple in treating the duplicity of humanity by showing that the decent Jekyll and the devilish Hyde are components of a single person and that the only way Jekyll can remove Hyde is by committing suicide. Hyde is the double of Jekyll. *Dorian Gray* is a longer and richer story with the issue of aestheticism as an absurd conception, which disillusions us about the value of beauty more than celebrates it. On the one hand, Dorian is completely addicted to the side of pleasure, not the other side, without which there is no pleasure. He indulges his lust and avoids the ugly or unpleasant side of life. On the other hand, however, the most significant issue is the motif of the *doppelgänger,* that is, the apparition/double of Dorian.

However, the *doppelgänger* theme is also a motif to lead us beyond language and thought. The picture that is identical to Dorian is certainly an altered quality of the concept of *doppelgänger,* another self. The picture torments Dorian, destroys his good nature, and culminates in his own death. While becoming immersed in the story, the reader comes to be placed in the Middle Path between morality and immorality.

It is reading as a pursuit of what lies beyond the thematic approach with the idea of poetic justice. Like *Dr. Jekyll and Mr. Hyde, Dorian Gray* does not end with vice (Hyde and the loathsome image of Dorian) being punished and virtue (Jekyll and the conscientious, good nature of Dorian) being rewarded. Nor does the text justify or heighten vice. Rather, in reading these Gothic texts, we become *pure* through fear as *affect.* Reading is experiencing the sublime through fear and insecurity, or *becoming pure* in Deleuze's terms.

From the perspective of Zen, the Gothic sublime you experience at the end of this Gothic novel has a form of *sudden awakening.* Until the last moment, the reader observes Dorian not accepting *dukkha,* that is, inevitable "suffering," "pain," or "unsatisfactoriness." Life is unsatisfactory because it always seemingly comprises transitory moments of the changing states of materials. Dorian wants to stop the change and have youth and beauty forever. Yet youth and beauty are mere phenomena, and the ultimate reality is Emptiness, or the Transmiddle Zone, the space of perfect liberty between the two sides of the binary opposition that forms one's perception of a phenomenon.

The new way of reading I propose is that this Gothic text is the process by which you go through the state of *disturbance* with irrational *kongans* and *hwadus* and eventually reach the point of enlightenment. The *hwadu* of this vast *kongan* would be, "What is it that eludes pleasure and pain?" The Buddhist *hwadu* "What is this?" is the question that you would ask yourself while reading the text. "What is this?" is the same as "What is the inexpressible goal that this text leads me to?" The imperceptible goal is not anything that can be found in the form of language or thought but the total outside.

Also, I would like to point out that, being immersed in this story, you come to experience *affect,* or the *sublime* sensibility, that emerges from the middle between the opposites (exteriority where there is no gross dual emotion—happiness and terror, like and dislike). The sublime sensibility arises in the *affective* Gothic mood. The decay of the beauty of Dorian in the picture tells you about his deteriorating moral sense. While reading this story, you do not need any traditionally oriented technique to interpret it with an excessively moral sense. The old theme of morality is an obstacle to this kind of understanding. The novel leads us beyond poetic justice. All you need is to follow the narration, which comprises binary oppositions—Dorian's success in pursuing sensuous pleasure and his moral degradation to abhorrence, young age and aging, the pursuit of pleasure and immorality. As we are led between the polar opposites, young and handsome looks on the one hand and old and loathsome looks on the other, we are pushed beyond both. Going beyond the binary opposition, you will experience the looming sense of *apathy*.

The *affective* quality of the novel leads you beyond the moral issue. Through the ongoing flow of the ego and its double, the Middle Path in Buddhist terms would be *affectively* looming over your mind without your conceptual knowing. It moves unknowingly because the middle zone is the ground of your true self without ego power. The moral issue seems too heavy and overwhelming, so the novel has been interpreted with the purity and moral law issue, but the focus should not be laid on it. The focus should be on Dorian's split ego. We go beyond language through the split.

The end breaks down the binary opposition, and you confront Dorian's death with the traces of his aging and of the sins and vices he has committed on his corpse (transferred from the painting). Both Dorian's handsome appearance and his sins/vices are now put in the right places, and this scene undeniably shocks the reader with vigorous power. Through the moment of fear, terror, and the loss of security, the Gothic sublime makes you look inside the ego and find the *emptiness* of immoral pleasure and moral tension. It is noticeable that Dorian's painting in itself already brings our attention to art, which deals with the reality of our emotions and affects. Through the Gothic sublime, the tension of your thoughts and feelings dissolve, and you come to encounter the heterogeneous otherness in yourself. Dorian's narcissistic self-image of youth and beauty has proven that nothing mystical is valuable.

The obstacle is the old theme of morality. You would see what is looming from beyond the conceptual moral issue, and it is not difficult for you to. Although moral judgment still lingers even after the end, the most important factor of reading is not the lesson that we have to live a moral life. You go through the process of *doubt* and reach the point of encountering the infinity of the exterior of the egoic judgment with reason and emotion, just as a Buddhist meditation practitioner experiences spiritual awakening that comes with great doubt. As in Buddhism, great doubt produces great enlightenment, and small doubt produces small enlightenment. The morality issue seems to be an obstacle that you must overcome. "Great doubt, great enlightenment; little doubt, little enlightenment; no doubt, no enlightenment" would make little sense for most traditional Tibetan lamas or Theravadin acharyas. Although the *Discourse to the Kalamas* reminds us of the value of doubt, the Indian tradition has not developed the theme of doubt any further.[66]

The picture of Dorian takes on a far greater role than that of a mirror. A mirror merely reflects the image of a person. However, the picture in this novel both takes on Dorian's aging and reflects his sensuous indulgence. It serves the novel by being both positive and negative toward Dorian's sensuous desire. It provides great momentum to lead us to the mystery of the novel—beyond poetic justice. As it deepens the polar opposites of young and old, handsome and loathsome, the picture leads us beyond them. Going beyond such binary opposition, you will experience the looming sense of *apathy*. Apathy comes at the limit of emotion, that is, in the last phase of the sublime. With the feeling of apathy or indifference comes the distancing of the true self from egoic attachment. As Nancy says, this feeling is not to be misunderstood with the ordinary meaning of "feeling." In fact, "it is not a feeling at all."[67] One could say that it is what remains of feeling at the limit, when feeling no longer feels itself, or when there is no longer anything to feel. It is still a feeling, but it rather detaches the reader from the emotions that directly derive from their experience of the reading. It is a sense of being alive both at the center of the presence of all phenomena and outside them, so to speak. The everlasting movement of truth is *the light* that dances within and without the limits of time and space.

5.4. The Gothic dance of light

At the end of *The Strange Case of Dr. Jekyll and Mr. Hyde,* Dr. Jekyll kills the loathsome Hyde, which means he commits suicide, and the novella leads us to the absence of both. The novella shows that Dr. Jekyll or the decent appearance of life and the violent aspect represented by Mr. Hyde are actually one. In *The Picture of Dorian Gray,* Dorian Gray pursues a sensuous life, which satisfies him with immediate happy feelings, and wishes to exclude the unsatisfying, unappetizing side of life. As he goes against the flow of time and destroys his image of aging and life's natural production of anxiety, pain, and ugliness, the unhoped-for side of life disappears as he wants. However, at the very same time, his youth and beauty also disappear, although he denies the fact and hides his picture that reflects it. At the end of the novel, the duality formed by the young, handsome Dorian Gray and the old, ugly Dorian Gray disappears. In both texts, what happens eventually is actually the destruction of the ego

---

[66] Stephen Batchelor, *The Faith to Doubt: Glimpses of Buddhist Uncertainty* (Berkeley: Counterpoint, 2015), 13.
[67] Nancy, "The Sublime Offering," 49.

construct of the protagonist and of the reader/viewer. As these examples and most, if not all, other literary texts show, the middle between the polar opposites guides us not to some phenomenal conclusion but to the exterior of the finite space of the story, or of language itself.

In the last analysis, these two *fin de siècle* Gothic novels, *Dr. Jekyll and Mr. Hyde* and *Dorian Gray*, are closer to *Moby-Dick* than *Hamlet* in the sense that they are both stories of removing the ego embodied in a concrete object. However, all these stories come to an end where we are truly ready to start meditation. The ultimate *hwadus* of these *kongans*, "What is this?" or "What am I?", raise strong doubts on the intensity of the sense of the egoic self in us, guiding us outside the circuit of the ego.

It is the dimension of the inconceivable that is ever explored both in Buddhism and in Western metaphysics. In this way, as your experiences of the Gothic sublime accumulate, the sensibility of the "don't-know mind" (the term often used by Seungsahn, the Korean Seon master widely known the world over), pure consciousness that is not known to the reasoning ego, will be directly and deeply felt as a spiritual feeling. Through this meditative reading, we have reached non-thinking or Emptiness without thinking about an object, and it is in fact the treasure of true wisdom to embrace both of the polar opposites of binary opposition! The sublime or *jouissance* we experience is the delight of being the true self, being *the freely dancing light.*

BIBLIOGRAPHY

Batchelor, Stephen. *The Faith to Doubt: Glimpses of Buddhist Uncertainty.* Berkeley: Counterpoint, 2015.

Bodri, William. *Socrates and the Enlightenment Path.* Boston: Red Wheel/Weiser, 2001.

Burke, Edmund. *A Philosophical Enquiry into the Origin of our Ideas of the Sublime and Beautiful.* Oxford: Oxford University Press, 1990.

Cleary, Thomas. *Entry Into the Inconceivable: An Introduction to Hua-Yen Buddhism.* Honolulu: University of Hawai'i Press, 1983.

Cleary, Thomas, trans. *The Flower Ornament Scripture: A Translation of the Avatamsaka Sutra.* Boston: Shambhala Publications, Inc., 1993.

Deleuze, Gilles and Felix Guattari. *A Thousand Plateaus: Capitalism and Schizophrenia.* Translated by Brian Massumi. Minneapolis: University of Minnesota Press, 1987.

Demiéville, Paul. "The Mirror of the Mind." In *Sudden and Gradual Enlightenment: Approaches to Enlightenment in Chinese Thought,* edited by Peter N. Gregory, 13-40. Honolulu: University of Hawai'i Press, 1987.

Derrida, Jacques. *Margins of Philosophy.* Translated by Alan Bass. Chicago: University of Chicago Press, 1982.

Donner, Neal. "Sudden and Gradual Intimately Conjoined: Chih-i's T'ien-t'ai View." In *Sudden and Gradual Enlightenment: Approaches to Enlightenment in Chinese Thought,* edited by Peter N. Gregory, 201-226. Honolulu: University of Hawai'i Press, 1987.

Foucault, Michel. "Language to Infinity." In *Language, Counter-memory, Practice: Selected Essays and Interviews by Michel Foucault,* edited by Donald F. Bouchard, 53-67. Ithaca: Cornell University Press, 1977.

Gasche, Rodolphe and Mark C. Taylor, eds. *Of the Sublime: Presence in Question.* Translated by Jeffrey S. Librett. Albany: State University of New York Press, 1993.

Gomez, Luis O. "Purifying Gold: The Metaphor of Effort and Intuition in Buddhist Thought and Practice." In *Sudden and Gradual Enlightenment: Approaches to Enlightenment in Chinese Thought,* edited by Peter N. Gregory, 67-165. Honolulu: University of Hawai'i Press, 1987.

Gottlieb, Anthony. *The Dream of Reason: A History of Western Philosophy.* New York: W. W. Norton & Company, 2016.

Harmless, S. J., William. *Mystics.* Oxford: Oxford University Press, 2008.

Heidegger, Martin. *Introduction to Metaphysics*. Translated by Gregory Fried and Richard Polt. New Haven: Yale University, 2000.

Humphries, Jeff. *Reading Emptiness: Buddhism and Literature*. Albany: State University of New York Press, 1999.

Iser, Wolfgang. *The Act of Reading: A Theory of Aesthetic Response*. Baltimore: Johns Hopkins University Press, 1978.

Bong, Joon-ho, dir. *Parasite*. 2019; Seoul: CJ Entertainment.

Kant, Immanuel. *Critique of Judgment*. Translated by Werner S. Pluhar. Indianapolis: Hackett Publishing Company, Inc., 1987.

LaVito, Angelica. "More Americans are meditating than ever before, as mindfulness goes mainstream." *CNBC*, November 8, 2018. https://headtopics.com/us/more-americans-are-meditating-than-ever-before-as-mindfulness-goes-mainstream-2397486.

Lee, Jae-seong. *Postmodern Ethics, Emptiness, and Literature: Encounters between East and West*. Lanham: Lexington Books, 2015.

Levinas, Emmanuel. *Totality and Infinity: An Essay on Exteriority*. Translated by Alphonso Lingis. Pittsburgh: Duquesne University Press, 1992.

Masci, David and Conrad Hackett. "Meditation is common across many religious groups in the U.S." *Pew Research Center*, January 2, 2018, https://www.pewresearch.org/fact-tank/2018/01/02/meditation-is-common-across-many-religious-groups-in-the-u-s/.

Melville, Herman. *Moby-Dick*. New York: Signet Classics, 2013.

Nancy, Jean-Luc. "The Sublime Offering." In *Of the Sublime: Presence in Question*, edited by Rodolphe Gasche and Mark C. Taylor, translated by Jeffrey S. Librett, 25-53. Albany: State University of New York Press, 1993.

Nietzsche, Friedrich. *The Will to Power*. Translated by Michael A. Scarpitti and R. Kevin Hill. New York: Penguin, 2017.

Phillips, Todd. *Joker*. 2019; Burbank, CA: Warner Bros. Pictures.

Rosenberg, Larry. *Three Steps to Awakening: A Practice for Bringing Mindfulness to Life*. Boston: Shambhala, 2013.

Smith, Daniel W. "Introduction: 'A Life of Pure Immanence': Deleuze's 'Critique et Clinique' Project." In Gilles Deleuze, *Essays Critical and Clinical*, translated by Daniel W. Smith and Michael A. Greco, xi-liv. Verso: London, 1998.

Solovyov, Vladimir. *The Crisis of Western Philosophy (Against the Positivists)*. Translated and edited by Boris Jakim. Hudson: Lindisfarne Press, 1996.

Stevenson, Robert Louis. *Strange Case of Dr Jekyll and Mr Hyde and Other Tales* (Oxford World's Classics). Edited by Roger Luckhurst. Oxford: Oxford University Press, 2008.

Thich Nhat Hanh, *Awakening of the Heart: Essential Buddhist Sutras and Commentaries.* Berkeley: Parallax Press, 2012.

Wilde, Oscar. *The Picture of Dorian Gray.* Edited by Norman Page. Peterborough: Broadview Press Ltd., 1998.

Zuckerman, Arthur. "46 Meditation Statistics: 2019/2020 Benefits, Market Value & Trends." *CompareCamp.com*, May 22, 2020. https://comparecamp.com/meditation-statistics/.

INDEX